THAT
WE
MAY
BE
ONE

THAT WE MAY BE ONE

A GAY MORMON'S PERSPECTIVE ON FAITH & FAMILY

TOM CHRISTOFFERSON

DESERET
BOOK

SALT LAKE CITY, UTAH

Library of Congress Cataloging-in-Publication Data

Names: Christofferson, Tom, author.
Title: That we may be one : a gay Mormon's perspective on faith and family / Tom Christofferson.
Description: Salt Lake City, Utah : Deseret Book, [2017] | Includes bibliographical references.
Identifiers: LCCN 2017025630 | ISBN 9781629723914 (paperbound)
Subjects: LCSH: Homosexuality—Religious aspects—The Church of Jesus Christ of Latter-day Saints. | Mormon gays. | Christofferson, Tom. | The Church of Jesus Christ of Latter-day Saints—Doctrines. | Mormon Church—Doctrines.
Classification: LCC BX8643.H65 C47 2017 | DDC 261.8/35766—dc23
LC record available at https://lccn.loc.gov/2017025630

Printed in the United States of America
Lake Book Manufacturing, Inc., Melrose Park, IL

10   9   8   7   6   5   4   3   2   1

For my incomparable parents,
Paul Vickery Christofferson and Leah Jeanne Swenson,
who have been and remain the foundational blessing of my life

And now Father, I pray unto thee for them,
and also for all those who shall believe on their words,
that they may believe in me,
that I may be in them as thou, Father, art in me,
that we may be one.

—3 NEPHI 19:23

Contents

Publisher's Preface

Among the many important books that we present each year, the uniqueness of this particular volume seems to invite a word of introduction from the publisher. It is a book that is both timely and needed by individuals, family members, and ward brothers and sisters who find themselves navigating one of the more difficult and emotionally intense topics of our time.

In this book, Tom Christofferson speaks from his heart. In doing so, he allows us to travel with him on a journey—a unique journey, because it is his and his alone, but one filled with insight and learning for all who are striving to understand and love their fellow man more fully and completely. In many ways, Tom's story is a love story. It is a story that recounts the love of parents for children, of children for parents, of siblings for each other, and of Saints, leaders, and members in the Lord's Church for one another.

Everyone who has worked on this project has witnessed Tom's gracious acknowledgment of the difficulties inherent in creating a book such as this one. His willingness to accept the risk of having his choices second-guessed and his motives misconstrued is testament to his desire to help others. And this book will help. It opens new dimensions to the dialogue about homosexuality and other gender-related issues that are so prevalent in today's society—and that result in very real questions among Church members.

The fact is, there is so much that we simply don't know. Where does homosexuality originate? Why does it even exist? What are its causes? For Latter-day Saints, who acknowledge the central role of marriage and family in our Heavenly Father's plan of salvation, those questions become even more poignant, complex, and heart-wrenching: What choices do those who identify as gay or lesbian have if they wish to remain faithful to gospel covenants? What is our Father's plan for these individuals in the eternities?

Although we recognize that not every LGBTQ individual's experience will mirror Tom's, we hope that his contribution to the dialogue will open doors and offer perspectives that readers may not have considered. Charity, the pure love of Christ, should, after all, be a universal experience among the family of God.

Introduction

I sat in my car in front of the bishop's house, too early to go to the door and too embarrassed to drive around the neighborhood one more time. It was a winter evening early in 2008. I had moved to New Canaan the previous summer. My partner and I had looked at a number of homes (it felt like we had looked at *every* house for sale in the lower Fairfield County area of Connecticut) before settling on the one at Four Winds Lane. I had felt drawn to the area because a long-ago BYU roommate of mine had lived in New Canaan, and I knew there was a ward there. As we were looking for homes we would often drive past the LDS chapel—the first time, my realtor pointed it out and said, "That's the Mormon church. They're good customers; lots of kids, so they buy big houses."

This meeting tonight would represent a significant step, one I had been contemplating for several months, ever since I had begun attending sacrament meetings frequently. On those Sunday mornings, I tried to time my arrival at the chapel to be about five minutes after the service had begun. I would sit in the back, in the overflow area in the cultural hall on those miserably uncomfortable steel folding chairs, and bolt for the door the moment I heard the "amen" of the benediction. But in that intervening hour, I felt the stirrings of something familiar, the Spirit-to-spirit confirmation of doctrine and testimony.

This would be my first formal conversation with a Church leader since I had left the Church more than twenty years earlier.

In 1984, I had been living in Southern California. My short-lived marriage to a wonderful woman, who had no way of understanding the havoc that marrying a man who thought he had "tendencies" would bring into her life, would soon be annulled. I felt I had tried in every way I knew how to be the "perfect" Mormon boy and man: president of every class and quorum, a love- and testimony-filled mission to Montreal, Québec, a degree from BYU, and marriage in the Los Angeles Temple. And yet, despite hours of prayers, days of fasting, years of service, I was still gay. I had reached the breaking point; I felt I couldn't keep moving in the direction I had been going. I had no concept that one could be gay *and* Mormon, and it felt important to me to feel I was approaching the next phase of my life with integrity, not trying to hide what I had come to know about myself. So I asked to be excommunicated in order that I could set out to discover if I could be gay *and* happy. At that time, simply identifying oneself as gay was sufficient reason for excommunication, so the council was brief and the result unsurprising.

Indeed, I had been blessed with a very happy life. An interesting and rewarding career had allowed me to live and work in Los Angeles, New York, Luxembourg, San Francisco, and London. In San Francisco, I met the man who would be my partner of nineteen years. He was a hospital administrator who would later qualify to be a family medicine doctor—a kind, smart, funny, generous, and thoughtful person who would become beloved of my parents, siblings, and nieces and nephews.

But two decades after leaving the Church, despite that enjoyable and fulfilling life, I felt the lack of a strong spiritual center.

My partner and I had attended a number of churches over time, and many embodied an admirable gospel of Christian action in the world, but they were missing the theology of the Restoration, so important to me. As a teenager, I had received a witness of the Book of Mormon, and that conviction had never left me. Wise parents had managed the process of ensuring that my partner and I were fully integrated into the family, so I had no feelings of anger, bitterness, or pride to keep me from acting on the desire to return to some kind of participation in church—the LDS church—to the degree possible.

And so, here I was, waiting for the clock to inch forward so that I could knock on the door of this bishop I had not met, waiting to ask him if I would be welcome to attend the meetings of his ward as a gay man in a long-standing monogamous relationship. Waiting to introduce myself as a man who had felt spiritual strength in that ward and wanted to experience those feelings more consistently, more powerfully, and to grow in knowledge and understanding of the things of God. I silently uttered another prayer, that whatever would be the right answer to help me along my journey would be made known to this bishop. In that moment, I did not yet realize that the Lord had put into my path a man whose professional experiences, whose comprehension of the gospel of Jesus Christ, and whose boundless heart would make him precisely the right person to open the doors for the next stage of my journey, for the unanticipated joy we together would be granted.

This book is my attempt to describe my perspective, how I have tried to follow impressions of the Spirit, and how I have experienced the presence of the Savior in my life. Please understand that I share this not as a prescription for others, rather as an appreciation for the life I have been allotted. My hope is that in the experiences and actions of my parents, family, and ward members, we all may find ideas about how as families and as a church we might more fully follow the example of Christ: "And ye see that I have commanded that none of you should go away, but rather have commanded that ye should come unto me, that ye might feel and see; even so shall ye do unto the world" (3 Nephi 18:25).

Some Thoughts on Language

"A happy gay Mormon." That's the shorthand I often use to describe myself. Some of my gay friends—as well as some of my LDS friends—are a little surprised that I think it's possible to be a gay Mormon. Perhaps it would be helpful to explain what I mean when I use this language.

To me, *gay* is a word I use to encompass some core elements of how I see and engage the world, the romantic pull I feel, and where the depth and breadth of relationships I form arise, the yearnings of my heart to connect with a unique other, to love and be loved, "time's best jewel," as Shakespeare described it.

In my usage of the term, some who feel this pull toward members of their own gender may also have sexual relations with them, and some may not. I am now, and have been for several years, in that latter category.

My eternal identity is as the child of Heavenly Parents. I have many other identities, some infinite, some only for this time. I am a man of primarily Scandinavian origins, an American, by profession a banker, a youngest son of superlative parents, a Christian, a Mormon, gay.

To me, the descriptor *same-sex attracted* fails to convey a sufficiently broad understanding. If you are a "straight" person, happily married to your companion, does the word *attraction* convey the depth of your feeling? Or, more likely, is it just a tiny, albeit happy, portion of the whole of your relationship?

I have other friends who prefer that term *(SSA)* for the very reason that it does not convey a consistent cultural meaning. Some are in the process of gaining an individual sense of what this facet of themselves will come to mean over time, and using the term *SSA* may allow space and time to integrate or negate a more specific identity. Some think *gay* carries a meaning overly specific and thus inapplicable to their lives.

So, while I prefer the descriptor *gay* (and appreciate its synonymous meanings of cheerful and lively), my practice when speaking to others of my tribe is to try to use the words they find most meaningful to them in describing this experience or identity. In this book, I will primarily use *gay* and *LGBTQ* to describe my experience and community.

By the way, the letters keep multiplying: the most inclusive current formulation of this community of interest is LGBTQIA: Lesbian, Gay, Bisexual, Transgender, Queer, Intersex, and Asexual. This formulation is meant to encompass both sexual orientation and gender identity. The current generation often favors *queer* over *gay* because it includes the notion of a sexual identity that is anything or everything other than *straight* and because it also incorporates broader, and perhaps more fluid, expressions of gender identity.

This is probably a good moment for a disclaimer: I write and speak from the perspective of my personal experience. Others can much more eloquently and more helpfully portray their journeys, especially as concerns gender identity. I hope an LDS writer will take up the task to educate all of us on the challenges, nuances, and joys of life in which gender clarity cannot be taken for granted.

I often hear, "I want to reach out more to LGBT brothers and sisters, but I'm afraid I'll say something offensive without knowing it and certainly without meaning it!" May I suggest, if that is your feeling, that you simply begin your conversation by expressing that feeling? Few things open doors of understanding more effectively than an honest acknowledgment of the desire to be taught. Your open heart will have the same effect on the persons with whom you speak: they will want to reciprocate your kindness and your interest. So, please don't be afraid to speak to any of your brothers and sisters. Just give them the chance to know your heart, and you might be surprised not only that no offense is taken but that your new friend will also want to better understand your experiences and perspective!

One other comment about language: if someone mentioned "the straight lifestyle," would that mean anything to you? I'm guessing the answer is "no" because you might feel there are as many different approaches to living life as there are straight people. When someone speaks about "the gay lifestyle," I ask them if they mean the nineteen-year monogamous relationship I had, or perhaps they mean the lives of my friends Sean and Randy, who married last year at the request of their daughter (the youngest of the three at-risk kids they've adopted). Sean is a prominent national politician and Randy has a successful multimedia design business. My point is that LGBTQ people are individuals with unique lives; some live in big cities, some are in the suburbs, and some are farmers. We can be far more effective in our communications if we talk about behaviors, such as promiscuous and monogamous, drug-addicted and abstemious, unbelieving and converted. All of those words can accurately describe behaviors of people in the LGBTQ community—and of people in the straight community.

Throughout my life, scientists and others have attempted to answer the question, "Why am I gay?" Nature vs. nurture, DNA, biology, chemistry of the womb, and practically numberless other theories have been proposed. It isn't a question I can answer, either. I find two phrases from the current version of the Church's website "Mormon and Gay" (mormonandgay.lds.org) as helpful as any others: "The experience of same-sex attraction is a complex reality for many people," and "individuals do not choose to have such attractions."

In my view, we are unlikely in this life to ever fully have all the answers we seek, but we always know the first and second great commandments (see Matthew 22:36–40). And when we understand that "charity is the pure love of Christ" (Moroni 7:47), we find both purpose and incentive to let go of ideas that being gay equals a lack of faith or an unwillingness to do hard work, that parents are at fault if children are gay, or that persons with such attractions are enemies of God.

Being gay is to me not simply an attraction, nor does it necessarily refer to sexual behavior—it is itself a way of being, an existence, an identity, a way of relating to the world and expressing one's existence. Being Mormon is also a way of being and relating to the world and expressing identity. So being gay *and* Mormon is a doubly rich existence for me—a unique way of being, existing, relating to the world, and sharing the light, love, intelligence, and truth of God and my relationship to Him.

PART ONE

———

LIVING

IN

REALITY

CHAPTER 1

Beginning

Apart from the pulling and hauling stands what I am,
Stands amused, complacent, compassionating, idle, unitary,
Looks down, is erect, or bends an arm on an impalpable certain rest,
Looking with side-curved head curious what will come next,
Both in and out of the game and watching and wondering at it.

Backward I see in my own days where I sweated through fog with
linguists and contenders,
I have no mockings or arguments, I witness and wait.

—WALT WHITMAN

I broke the news to my parents by phone. I was living in California, and their home was in Colorado. I had tried out various ways of announcing that I was separating from my wife, and finally found one I thought would head off at least a few questions. But the core question wasn't going to be avoided—"why?"—and the only answer I had was, "because I'm gay." The other end of the line was very quiet, and finally my mother said, "Well, I guess we've always known."

I guess I had always known too, or at least from about age five, when I didn't have language to describe it. What I did have was a profound sense that I was different from my four older

3

brothers in an important but not-to-be-talked-about way. In junior high school, I looked up the word *homosexual* in the library dictionary, my heart pounding in my ears, afraid someone would look over my shoulder and learn what had just been confirmed to me.

I lived my teen years with a sort of split personality: going through the experiences that form a testimony of the Book of Mormon and of the restored Church of Jesus Christ while also harboring clandestine crushes and feeling that the secret I was hiding disconnected me from the very God I was just coming to know.

I recall junior high school with a shudder of revulsion. The school was composed of only the seventh and eighth grades and had about twelve hundred students. As far as I can now recall, I was the only Mormon in my year—certainly the only one in any of my classes. I wasn't athletic, and I was an uneven student, excelling in areas that interested me (which did not include math or science). My elementary school friends were all in other classes, so I was something of a loner. I lived for Wednesdays and Fridays, and dreaded Mondays. What we then called MIA (which we now call Mutual) met every Wednesday evening, and for those brief hours I was surrounded by friends and felt like I fit in, even though I wasn't a particularly enthusiastic Scout. On weekends I was with my family, and on Sundays with friends at church. Sunday evenings were a torture of dread that the despised Monday was nigh again.

Reading the Book of Mormon each morning together with my family before leaving for school was a great solace and comfort to me. As dreary as the day might be, I had things to ponder from our reading. That was when I first recall coming across Nephi's promise: "And it came to pass that I, Nephi, said unto my father: I will go and do the things which the Lord hath commanded, for I know that the Lord giveth no commandments unto the children of men, save he shall prepare a way for them that they may accomplish the thing which he commandeth them" (1 Nephi 3:7). It was the first scripture I memorized, and I felt its power in the external part of my life, surviving junior high school, and in the internal part, where I was waging the battle to know how not to be gay.

During these years, my dad was effectively working two jobs—fulfilling his normal position in the Chicago office of a veterinary pharmaceutical firm as well as running the company's Denver production site—and serving as a stake high councilor. Most weeks, he would work in the Chicago office on Monday, fly to Denver on Tuesday, and return home to Chicago late Friday evening. In those pre-9/11 days, it was possible to go to the gate of arriving domestic passengers and greet them there. My brother Tim was in his freshman year at BYU when I was in seventh grade, and then on his mission to Brazil when I was in eighth grade, so the Friday evening trips to O'Hare Airport were often just Mom, Wade, and me (or, if Wade had a date, Mom and me). I remember those trips to and from the airport fondly as a time for catching up and just being together. I think Dad was living in a state of perpetual fatigue those two years, but somehow being in the car always brought out his fun side.

Let me digress for a moment to talk about family car trips. When I was three, we moved to northern New Jersey, and then when I was nine to the suburbs of Chicago. Both sets of grandparents lived in Utah, so every summer we would bundle in the car and drive to Utah. Interstate 80 was not yet complete across the whole country, so there were some stretches where the road was only one lane in each direction. Long tailbacks of cars could build up behind tractor-trailers, waiting for the opportunity to pass. One of those sections of not-yet-completed interstate was outside Sydney, Nebraska. Dad's goal on these trips was to overnight in Sydney and get on the road as early as possible the next morning "to get ahead of the trucks." As I recall, he did all the driving, and we would normally drive for sixteen hours or so each day. In the first few summer trips, that meant we had the five boys and two parents in either a station wagon or a sedan. In July. Without air conditioning. Proper timing of meals and toilet breaks became an art that Dad would have preferred to have been a science. "Did you go to the bathroom?" was the greeting as each person got back in the car after a meal or refueling. It came as a great surprise to him that a five-year-old who didn't need to use the restroom when the car was getting gasoline could suddenly have a dire need ten miles down the road.

On these road trips, as evening came on and Dad became increasingly tired, he would begin to sing the songs he had learned as a young boy in Lehi to keep himself awake. "Fourth Ward Trailbuilders Can't Be Beat" and "Tobacco Is a Filthy Weed" were frequent favorites that we all came to memorize.

We all slept in one motel room on these trips. The great secret was to get to sleep before Dad did. I have inherited at least that one trait of his: when I'm exceptionally tired, my snoring can shake the foundations of sturdy buildings. I remember one evening, in a not-really-great-smelling motel room in Sydney, Nebraska, when Wade and I hadn't managed to beat Dad to slumber. A few moments later, I heard Wade loudly say what until then we had heard only Mother plead: "Roll over, Sweetheart!"

To continue with the story of my teenage years: It was in junior high that I first recall anyone calling me a "homo." It was in gym class, where I was playing basketball—poorly. I had figured out by then that I was indeed homosexual, had found the definition in the library's enormous copy of the *Oxford English Dictionary,* but it was the secret I most wanted to hide. Looking back, I don't know if the slur was because I was such a miserably unskilled basketball player or if there were other signs, but I became obsessed over whether I walked like a straight guy or rolled my hips too much, if I talked like a straight guy or had a sibilant "s," if my voice was deep enough, if I moved my hands the "right" way.

My parents knew that I hated school, in spite of getting overall good grades; they knew that church and home were my refuge. My constant prayer was that I could just get through the junior high experience and that something better would be apparent at the other end. I know my parents were praying for me too, that somehow this time would be of benefit to me.

In any event, as Wade graduated from high school and I from junior high school, Dad decided to go back into a large-animal private veterinary practice. Before accepting the position with Squibb that had taken us to New Jersey, Dad had been Utah's state veterinarian, and in that capacity he had traveled all over the state. One particular area, around Delta, had interested him, and through the years he had kept track of the dairies and feedlots there. He judged that the time was right for Delta and the surrounding communities to be able to support their own vet. And so, that summer, we left the big city behind and traveled to that small town of about 2,500 people in central Utah. A popular television program of the time, *Petticoat Junction,* featured a tiny town with colorful characters. I thought we had landed on the set of that show. Pretty quickly, though, I came to love the town and its ordinary people, as well as its characters, and I count lifelong friends from the years spent there.

I loved attending church in Delta and, thankfully, enjoyed attending high school as well. I found my peers to be readily accepting and welcoming of the new kid. I had the experience, as so many others have had, of blossoming in a small school and discovering the joy that talented teachers have in nurturing the gifts and interests of their students.

Because Dad was no longer traveling, and I was now the only son at home, my parents and I had a lot of time together and developed close friendships. After twenty-five years or so of cooking for six males, Mom was quite happy to have help in the kitchen. She had undergone radical cancer surgery a few months after I was born, and during the years following that surgery, all of my brothers, especially Todd and Wade, had become excellent bread bakers, and Tim was a great pie maker. All of us learned to do our own laundry and housecleaning, so my brothers were good catches when they married! I liked to cook and especially enjoyed trying new recipes modeled after those of my sister-in-law MarJane, Greg's wife, who I thought was the epitome of culinary ability and social pacesetting in general.

I loved how I felt at church and seminary as I began to feel the stirrings of the Spirit. I appreciated the sense of belonging to something that really mattered, of having access to knowledge that the rest of the world was either looking for or had decided to ignore. I especially began to feel closer to loving Heavenly Parents. "O My Father" was my favorite hymn, and I found particularly poignant the lines:

In the heav'ns are parents single?
No, the thought makes reason stare!
Truth is reason; truth eternal
Tells me I've a mother there.

I knew what it was like to have devoted, caring, wise earthly parents, and so it has been easier for me, perhaps, than for some whose parental relationship has been more challenging, to feel connected to eternal parents. This is a gift and blessing in my life, and I count myself extremely fortunate to possess it.

———

CHAPTER 2

Goodly Parents

The joys of parents
are secret;
and so are
their griefs and fears.

—Francis Bacon

In order to help you understand the journey my parents took along with their gay son, may I share with you some elements of their lives?

My father, Paul V. Christofferson, was a veterinarian by profession, and during most of my life his talents were focused on research and development of veterinary pharmaceuticals. He was the first person in his family to attend college, the first to earn an advanced degree. He was raised in Lehi, Utah, the fourth of his father's nine children who would live to adulthood. Dad's mother died of pneumonia when he was eight. That wasn't something he talked about much, although I remember a time being out with him when he was vaccinating cattle, and he showed me a syringe of penicillin and said, "This shot could have saved my mother's life." Having lost his mother at such a young age made him, I think, particularly sensitive to the role of the mother in a family.

My brothers and I recall nothing that would get my generally calm and even-tempered father angry more quickly than if we disrespected our mother!

Our mother, Leah Jeanne Swenson, was born in Pleasant Grove, Utah, and raised in the Manila neighborhood of that town, composed largely of Swedish and Danish immigrants, many of whom were her relatives. Her father, Helge Vincent Swenson, was perhaps the saintliest person I have ever known. He was gentle and soft-spoken, always kind and gracious, with a quiet but quick wit and an unwavering commitment to the gospel of Jesus Christ. Knowing his history, I have often wondered how he retained such a benevolent nature, despite a difficult early life. He was eight when his family emigrated from Sweden to Utah, but as they were to board the ship, the captain raised the fare, and they no longer had enough money to take the whole family. The older children were needed to work and help the family get by when they arrived in their new home; the younger children required care. My grandfather, as the middle child, was left behind to stay with his grandparents, who, angry at the decision of their child, were abusive and unkind to young Helge, according to my mother. Three years later, the funds were finally available for him to join his family, although he was able to spend only one night with them in their dugout sod home before going out to work for and board with various other families.

One lesson our grandfather helped teach us was about the importance and privilege of prayer. My brother Todd remembers:

> In 1960, I was fifteen and I will always be glad that I could help Grandpa Swenson as much as I did on the farm that summer. He was seventy-six years old at the time, and although still vigorous, any of the physical

11

work that I could handle was a real help to him. I felt that in that way I repaid a few cents worth of my great debt to him. I recall one morning that summer I was slow getting out of bed for the morning chores when he called downstairs to wake me. When he came down later to see why I was not at breakfast, he found me on my knees beside the bed offering a morning prayer. He did not interrupt, but waited outside the bedroom door until I had finished. As I stood up, he came into the room. There was no criticism for my having stayed in bed too long. Instead, he took me in his arms and told me how thrilled he was to find me in prayer. He spoke movingly for a moment about the privilege of talking with our Heavenly Father in prayer. He expressed his love for me and then went back upstairs while I got dressed. From that moment, I have never doubted the efficacy and importance of prayer. From his conviction, so honestly and lovingly expressed, I drew a new understanding and appreciation of that sacred privilege which has remained with me ever since.

My mother was his fifth and youngest child, and he was called into the bishopric of the Manila Ward six months after she was born. He served as a counselor and then bishop until six months before she was married.

Her brother Calvin recalled this of their father:

Through one particular instance, Father impressed upon my mind that the gospel is our greatest treasure. We were planting a new fruit orchard. He picked out a few of the best young trees and told me Brother Monson might like a few to plant. Father asked me to take them to him. But I was exasperated: "Father," I said, "I don't understand why we must always take the best bucketful of cherries, the best box of peaches and the best load of hay—and the best of everything else—to Brother Monson. I don't even think he is a very good man. He doesn't live the Word of Wisdom, he doesn't come to Church, and he seems to plan to have his berry pickers working in the patch right across from the chapel on Sundays. I don't know why you do anything for him." I will never forget my father's quiet answer; "Yes, son," he replied, "I know he has these habits that keep him from the Church. I'm sorry about that and keep praying that he will change. But he is the missionary who brought the gospel to my parents' home in Sweden. What he chooses to do is his responsibility. But all that I can ever to do show my love and appreciation for him can never be enough to pay for the priceless gift of the gospel that he brought into my life."

My father also taught us to give wholeheartedly to any Church calling we may have. Many a Sunday dinner was delayed while we waited for Father. Whenever he was responsible for the Aaronic Priesthood, or was a teacher of a class, before coming home he would go to the homes of any members who had been absent to find out why, and assure them that the member had been missed and was needed. My father taught us with his love and his life.

This heritage of whole-hearted conversion to the gospel of Jesus Christ and a home filled with "gentleness and meekness, and . . . love unfeigned" (Doctrine and Covenants 121:41) was the birthright of my mother. It guided the way she instilled in her sons everything important in life.

Our parents met at BYU when Mom was a freshman and Dad a newly returned missionary from the Southern States Mission (where his father had also served). They met at a dance, and one of my favorite pictures of them is at their sixtieth wedding anniversary, sharing a dance and a kiss.

They were married in January 1944. The nation had been at war for two years, and Dad had been accepted into the Army's Veterinary Corps, which allowed him to begin studies for his Doctor of Veterinary Medicine degree. He served in Asia, largely in Burma, working with pack animals being flown over "the Hump," the air support of China. His younger brother, David, was a tail gunner of a "flying fortress" bomber; his aircraft was shot down, and David was lost at sea. My oldest brother was named David Todd in his honor. Born while Dad was overseas, Todd was nearly a year old when he first met his father, now returned from war. My second brother, Greg, was born in Fort Collins, Colorado, while Dad was completing his degree at Colorado State University. The family moved to Utah when Dad began practicing veterinary medicine, and my brothers Tim and Wade and I were all born in Utah County.

From our earliest years, we were witnesses to the love and loyalty that existed between our parents. In a general priesthood session of conference, Todd related the following experience:

> Years ago, when my brothers and I were boys, our mother had radical cancer surgery. She came very close to death. Much of the tissue in her neck and shoulder had

to be removed, and for a long time it was very painful for her to use her right arm.

One morning about a year after the surgery, my father took Mother to an appliance store and asked the manager to show her how to use a machine he had for ironing clothes. The machine was called an Ironrite. It was operated from a chair by pressing pedals with one's knees to lower a padded roller against a heated metal surface and turn the roller, feeding in shirts, pants, dresses, and other articles. You can see that this would make ironing (of which there was a great deal in our family of five boys) much easier, especially for a woman with limited use of her arm. Mother was shocked when Dad told the manager they would buy the machine and then paid cash for it. Despite my father's good income as a veterinarian, Mother's surgery and medications had left them in a difficult financial situation.

On the way home, my mother was upset: "How can we afford it? Where did the money come from? How will we get along now?" Finally Dad told her that he had gone without lunches for nearly a year to save enough money. "Now when you iron," he said, "you won't have to stop and go into the bedroom and cry until the pain in your arm stops." She didn't know he knew about that. I was not aware of my father's sacrifice and act of love for my mother at the time, but now that I know, I say to myself, "There is a man."

I have shared these stories about my parents' traditional Mormon background to explain why it was no easier for them to have a gay son than it would be for any other LDS parent.

Yet they showed extraordinary compassion, empathy, and open-mindedness toward me, in spite of their own difficulty and struggles to understand me.

It was in the Reagan era of the mid-1980s, and AIDS was making the news with images of fear and dread about gay men, when my parents encountered the reality of my gay orientation. They took time to discover how best to respond after I came out to them. Gratefully, they anchored their lives equally to their rock-solid commitment to the gospel of Jesus Christ and to their love for every member of their family.

My brother Greg recalls this time:

> Tom called me from Los Angeles one day in July, 1984, while my wife and I were at a company retreat in La Jolla, California. He said he wanted to come talk with me immediately, so he drove to La Jolla. He told me that his marriage had ended and was going to be annulled because he was gay. Seeing his obvious distress and knowing his wife and her family well, I thought that all could be resolved if I could find a way to help Tom get "fixed," to change his sexual orientation from homosexual to heterosexual.
>
> A few days later I visited a friend who was at that time the head of LDS Social Services for Southern California. I explained my goal to him and asked who he would recommend as a counselor to help Tom "change." He responded, "Greg, of all of the homosexual men in this world, what group do you think would want more than any other to change their sexual orientation? LDS gay men, because of our doctrine and emphasis on the family and children. I will tell you that I have counseled

more than 400 gay LDS men, most of whom desperately wanted to change their sexual orientation, and very, very few have felt they were successful at doing so."

My understanding completely changed in those few minutes with my friend. There was nothing to "fix" about Tom. This was who he was—the same brother I had always loved—and he still had the wonderful personality and Christlike attributes that made him who he was. I discussed what I had learned with my wife. Her response was, "Tom lived with us before he was married. Let's be sure he knows he can come live with our family again if he needs to."

The sage advice from Greg's friend, although it offered little hope of change, actually helped my parents move on a practical course, recognizing the realities of the situation.

My parents' initial reaction when I came out had been to try to identify what they had done wrong. For a period, my father was convinced that I was gay because he had spent so much time traveling for work and had not been present often enough as I was growing up. My parents wondered what they could have done differently so that I would not be gay. As with Greg in the recollection just shared, they also wondered what they could do to "fix" me. For some time they used every fast Sunday, and invited other family members to join, fasting and praying that the Lord would heal me, that He would "take away the gay" from my life.

As with many LDS parents in similar circumstances, they had to mourn the dreams they had for me, especially that I would have a wife and children and that the Church would retain the central place in my life. When I asked to be excommunicated, it was from a sense that I needed to be honest about my life and that the only way I could do so was to move forward on a different path. Although that came as a relief for me, at least for a time, it was a very hard blow to them, and likely one that felt like a personal repudiation of that which they held so dear. There was a period—thankfully, a short one—during which communication was difficult between us, and both understanding and tempers were short.

It was not an instant thing for them, but progressively over the first couple of years they seemed to gain peace that the Lord was aware of me. They came to feel they could leave much of this in His hands.

About two years after I had come out, my family was planning a weeklong family reunion at a cabin in the canyon. I was living in Los Angeles and had a boyfriend at the time, and I said the two of us would be happy to come. Now, to be fully transparent, let me say that my boyfriend had absolutely no interest in attending, but I thought it was important to make a political statement that I wasn't going to come if this man I was dating wasn't also invited. My brothers all had young children, and some felt uncomfortable about how to handle this—to the extent that one family thought they might not bring their children if my boyfriend were present. My parents, attempting to broker a solution, finally said to me, "Will you please come, this once, by yourself for two days so that we can have a family council meeting the first evening?" I agreed.

That night, after the grandchildren had been put to bed, my brothers, their wives, my parents, and I gathered in the largest bedroom to speak. We began with prayer, and then, as I recall, my father talked about the importance of unity and loyalty to one another. My mother said, "I'm ashamed to say it, but there was a time when I thought we were the perfect Mormon family. I have this picture in my head of when Dad was called as bishop in New Jersey and the local paper sent a photographer for the story. You boys were wearing your bow ties, and I thought we really had it all figured out, that we were the perfect Mormon family. But then life happens, and I realized that there is no perfect Mormon family. The only thing we can really be perfect at is loving each other." Then she addressed my brothers and sisters-in-law and said, "The most important lesson your children will learn from how our family treats their Uncle Tom is that nothing they can ever do will take them outside the circle of our family's love."

That became their guiding principle. As my parents said to my brother Wade around that time, "We don't understand or know how all of this will play out in eternity, so we are going to make sure we enjoy every single moment with Tom in this life." I think over the years they became more at ease with how eternity might play out. A few years before my mother passed away, she and my father and I were having a conversation during a drive when they had come to Connecticut for a visit. We talked about what we prayed for, with the hope that we might be united in our prayers. We agreed that we could pray in faith that the perfect Judge of us all, knowing our circumstances and the desires of our hearts, seeing all the things that we do not, would also know of our love for Him and for each other. We could pray that in His flawless wisdom and mercy, we would someday gain an understanding of how the plan of happiness will include me in its fulness.

I recall one conversation a few years ago with my father when I told him how much I loved him and how greatly I appreciated the charity and empathy he showed to me. He was quiet for a few moments and then said, "I've thought about what would have happened if I had gone home and told my father I was gay, and I'm very sure he would have thrown me out of the house and had nothing to do with me ever again." Then Dad said, "As I look at your brothers with their children, I think each generation gets better at parenting and learning to show our love."

A line from Yeats well describes my mother: "One with her are mirth and duty." She loved to laugh, and she particularly enjoyed telling stories at her own expense, such as the time when our family had recently moved to New Jersey and she was pleased to find a fruit orchard where she could acquire peaches for canning. The family who owned the orchard proudly and repeatedly told her of their brother, a Catholic Monseigneur. Undertaking the move to New Jersey was the farthest my mother had ever traveled from her Utah home, and likely only the third or fourth time she had left that state. Having no clue what a Monseigneur might be, but wanting to be friendly, she asked, "Oh, isn't that wonderful! And is he married?"

Mother once said that among the very favorite memories of her life were the times when all of her sons were together laughing, because she knew the bonds of love in her family were secure and eternal. I knew that she had arrived at a place of being comfortable about her gay son when I overheard her at church one Sunday when my partner and I were visiting. She had been complimented on a beautiful suit she was wearing, and I heard her say, "Oh you just need to get a gay son and then you'll have a wonderful wardrobe!"

CHAPTER 3

Thriving in Ambiguity

There is a tide in the affairs of men,
Which, taken at the flood, leads on to fortune;
Omitted, all the voyage of their life
Is bound in shallows and in miseries.
On such a full sea are we now afloat;
And we must take the current when it serves
Or lose our ventures.

—WILLIAM SHAKESPEARE

As a seminary student, in the year we were studying the Book of Mormon, I remember having a conversation with my dad about the literal accuracy of it: "Do you think every story in the Book of Mormon was recorded at the time and everything happened exactly as it says?" I asked. "Or do you think these are lessons meant to teach us about Christ and His dealings with His people for application in the lives of people today?"

Now, my brothers will tell you, our Dad was very knowledgeable about the gospel. He loved the scriptures and immersed himself in them regularly, could recite a surprisingly large number of verses from memory, and also loved to learn about the history of the Church and the growth of Joseph Smith's doctrinal understanding. He was also a very practical man: if you asked him a question, he gave you an answer. On this occasion, though, he was quiet for a few moments. Finally he said, "How do you feel about the Book of Mormon?" I said that I believed I had received the witness that Moroni speaks of in the tenth chapter, and that I was confident the book was a second witness of Jesus Christ. He said, "Would it make a difference to how you feel about it, if the book were accurate as a daily diary or if it were a moral guide, a metaphor to lead us to Christ?" Now it was my turn to be quiet and to ponder. "I guess not." That ended the conversation—although in the years since he has passed away, I have wished that I would have asked Dad the question again to hear his insights. I was satisfied with the response, and I think in many ways it allowed me to learn to think about the larger issues and not to become fixated with smaller details. I didn't need to have all the answers.

If you are the parent of an LGBTQ child, I think you will agree that we do not have all the answers we would like to have in this life. We don't know much about how being gay, for example, in mortality plays out in an eternal sense—the place of this particular child in the plan of salvation. A dear friend who is the mother of a gay son in his twenties once said to me, "I'm a convert to the Church. I was drawn to it because it had the answers to the questions in my heart. And now the most important questions I have are left for me to work out!" Joseph Smith has been quoted as saying; "There is no pain so awful as the pain of suspense."

The righteous desires of a parent's heart may entail a substantial requirement for faith, patience, and perseverance. The principles found in Joseph Smith's letter from Liberty Jail provide a model for how we can effectively reach out to a challenging child or to those who have, for whatever reason, become alienated from the Church: "No power or influence can or ought to be maintained by virtue of the priesthood, only by persuasion, by long-suffering, by gentleness and meekness, and by love unfeigned; by kindness, and pure knowledge, which shall greatly enlarge the soul without hypocrisy, and without guile" (Doctrine and Covenants 121:41–42).

When I told my parents that I did not see a place for myself within the Church, I know it was a severe blow to the hopes and dreams they held for my life. I had served an honorable mission, and they knew how deeply I loved the teachings of the gospel, which continued to resonate with me even when I felt at odds with the Church. As they struggled with how to respond, my parents concluded that the two most critical elements of their lives, their testimonies of the gospel of Jesus Christ and their love for their children, could only be fully realized together. Their faith was based on their understanding of eternal life, including eternal families, and their family's strength was found in the teachings of the Church. To leave either rock on which they had built their lives, faith or family, Church or children, was incomprehensible to them.

For a couple of decades when I chose not to have any involvement with the Church, as they listened to the promptings they were receiving, my parents focused on their enjoyment of our time together, ensuring that I was always included in family events. I know their constant prayer was that I would feel the desire to become active in the Church and to make the necessary decisions to allow that to occur. But I also felt that they liked me, they were genuinely interested in all elements of my life, and they wanted me to share my whole life with them. They weren't waiting for me to return to church before they could fully love me, and so through them I came to understand the meaning of unqualified love. More powerful than any sermon or lecture they could have given was their example of steadfastness, "by gentleness and meekness, and by love unfeigned": the family prayers I joined each evening when staying in their home, hearing that both my partner and I were included in those prayers, watching and listening to them read scriptures together before they would go to sleep, and the occasional shared spiritual experience—all conveyed their love and acceptance of their gay son.

I have reflected on the "kindness and pure knowledge" my parents displayed in how they piloted our family through this journey, and especially how markedly different their approach was from that of others in the same era. Although they provided absolute clarity in words and actions within our family, they took the approach of waiting to be asked by others outside the family before offering advice or sharing the wisdom they had gained. It strikes me that they held the revelations they received for their stewardship of their children to be both sacred and personal. Their reticence to trumpet the "right way" for *all* families to approach these challenges reflected their reluctance to impose upon the sacred space of any other parents' opportunities and obligations to hear Heavenly Father's counsel, reflecting His knowledge of the unique personalities and needs of those children.

My parents' willingness to walk in faith was deeply ingrained in them. And it allowed them to continue to walk without clarity of how, or if, their righteous desires would be fulfilled.

Their love for me erected no barriers. If I was interested in something, they were interested. I recall Dad asking me one night at a restaurant, when the four of us had gone to dinner during one of their visits to New York, what I had learned about wine and the differences between types and vintages. If I had not understood it before that night, I clearly learned that my father wanted to know me—not the person he hoped or wished I might be, but the person I had become. That, to me, is love unfeigned.

Some parents of LGBTQ children have told me that one thing they learned in the journey with their child is that our Heavenly Parents know that child best. In Their eternal family, we are brothers and sisters of those entrusted to us as children on this earth. In the understanding of a peer relationship, those parents have found it easier to live by faith in the wisdom and understanding of our shared Heavenly Parents and to embrace the gift of agency as an essential part of their child's mortal experience.

As in all things, the Savior provides us the clearest example of loving those whose life choices have been less than He would have hoped, allowing His kind acceptance and regard to show them a higher vision of their own possibilities than they had previously grasped. Such is the lesson of one of my favorite New Testament stories, involving the Samaritan woman at Jacob's Well. Author and educator Camille Fronk Olson made this insightful observation:

> Jesus did not commence the conversation by pointing out what the woman needed to change in order to recognize and follow him. Rather, he began by opening her eyes to possibilities that exceeded anything she could have imagined. When her problematic [life] was finally verbalized, instead of being offended, she reverenced the stranger even more. . . . "Sir," she immediately responded, "I perceive thou art a prophet (John 4:19)." . . .
>
> Life-changing revelation came to her, revelation as

profound as we find in scripture. But her conversion was not in the dramatic fashion of Alma the Younger or Saul on the road to Damascus. In a quiet and contemplative way, the Samaritan woman received a clear witness while in the midst of doing ordinary household chores. In her humble way, she therefore encourages any who feel disenfranchised to trust in the Lord's invitation to drink from his living water and experience his love and power to save them.

For the first time in His earthly ministry, to this woman with a blemished life, Christ unequivocally testified of Himself as the Messiah: "I that speak unto thee am he" (John 4:26). And unlike Nicodemus, who may also have understood that Jesus was the Messiah, who visited Him in the dark of night and went quietly away, this wonderful woman took the knowledge she had gained and shared the good news with all in her village, "And many of the Samaritans . . . believed on him for the saying of the woman, which testified, He told me all that I ever did. . . . And many more believed because of his own word; and said unto the woman, Now we believe, not because of thy saying: for we have heard him ourselves, and know that this is indeed the Christ, the Saviour of the world" (John 4:39, 41–42).

Through my parents' actions, I have gained additional understanding of the love of the Savior. Because of their unqualified love, I have at least in a small way begun to comprehend how the Father can offer helpful commandments and ensure agency is untrammeled. Seeing my parents' life of patient faith and their willingness to wait upon the Lord, I also have learned to trust His promises and rely on the invaluable gift of His Atonement.

Elder Richard G. Scott proposed to parents and Church

leaders: "As a companion to that love, trust them. In some cases it may seem difficult to trust, but find some way to trust them. The children of Father in Heaven can do amazing things when they feel trusted. Every child of God in mortality chose the Savior's plan. Trust that given the opportunity, they will do so again."

As lesbian, gay, bisexual, transgender, queer, or same-sex attracted members of the Church of Jesus Christ, we live in the reality of two independent, contradictory truths: first, that every element of who we are is known to our Father, and we are His beloved children; and second, that His prophets have said that what comes naturally to us, what feels like it is at the core of our being, must not find physical expression. I recognize that the situation for transgender brothers and sisters is slightly different and that the counsel is less clear—you have the most challenging path, and there are even fewer answers available to you currently. I am grateful for the trans people in my life: your courage, your patience, and your good humor beckon me, with my far lesser challenges, to aim higher in order to follow your valorous example. Thank you!

How will we go forward, what decisions will we make, what costs will we pay, and what grace and joy will we receive? Especially with Alma's words ringing in our ears, "For I ought to be content with the things which the Lord hath allotted unto me" (Alma 29:3). "Being content," as Elder Neal A. Maxwell expressed in his usual discerning manner, "means acceptance without self-pity. Meekly borne, however, deprivations . . . can end up being like excavations that make room for greatly enlarged souls."

As a teenager and a young adult I prayed that God would transform me into someone I imagined would be more acceptable to Him. I thought righteousness, as measured by scrupulously obeying every possible commandment (see Hebrews 10:1), would be my way of paying for such a miracle. I aspired to be the most diligent missionary ever in an attempt to earn the change I sought. I hoped marrying in the temple would persuade God that I was a faithful follower, and therefore He would, in effect, put a new intelligence, a new soul, into my body.

Clearly that is not His plan. But I learned to take comfort, as I hope all LGBTQ individuals and their loved ones will, in the Savior's words to His Apostles at the Last Supper as He was preparing them for the challenges they would yet face: "I will not leave you comfortless: I will come to you. . . . Peace I leave with you, my peace I give unto you: not as the world giveth, give I unto you. Let not your heart be troubled, neither let it be afraid" (John 14:18, 27).

CHAPTER 4

Daily Bread

These weary hours will not be lost,
These days of passive misery,
These nights of darkness anguish tos't
If I can fix my heart on Thee.

. . .

That secret labour to sustain
With humble patience every blow,
To gather fortitude from pain
And hope and holiness from woe.

. . .

If Thou shouldst bring me back to life
More humbled I should be;
More wise, more strengthened for the strife,
More apt to lean on Thee.

—ANNE BRONTË

How can we develop the capacity to live with ambiguity? How can we cope with the challenges placed before us in this life? I believe the Lord has a special way of tutoring us over time.

The general conference of October 1944 took place in the third year of America's active involvement in World War II,

29

about seven months before victory in Europe would be celebrated and ten months before the surrender of Japan. In the war then raging, more than 400,000 U.S. service members would be killed as well as ten times that number of German military personnel, and about 60 million civilians across the world would lose their lives, which equated to about 3 percent of the world's total population at the time. Against that backdrop, President Heber J. Grant said:

> I am praying with all my heart and soul for the end of this war as soon as the Lord can see fit to have it stop. And to those homes that have been sorrowed by the loss of loved ones through death, may the peace and understanding and comfort of our Father in heaven be there unfailingly. And to you who are bereaved by the cruelty of war, I say, do not look forward to a life of care and trouble and anxiety, but look only to the duties and responsibilities of a single day [see Matthew 6:34], and by performing the duties each day that rest upon you, the burdens will be lightened notwithstanding all the sorrow that may come into your lives and the many things that may be hard for you to bear.

Speaking more than twenty-five years later, President Harold B. Lee said: "Don't try to live too many days ahead. Seek for strength to attend to the problems of today. . . . Do all that you can do and leave the rest to God, the Father of us all."

And more recently, speaking at a Church Educational System fireside, Elder D. Todd Christofferson said: "Thoughtful planning and preparation are key to a rewarding future, but we do not live in the future—we live in the present. It is day by day that we work out our plans for the future; it is day by day that we achieve our goals. It is one day at a time that we raise and nurture our families. It is one day at a time that we overcome imperfections. We endure in faith to the end one day at a time. It is the accumulation of many days well lived that adds up to a full life and a saintly person."

The insight these apostles and prophets have shared is, I believe, a manner by which the Lord sustains and trains all of His children. When Jesus taught his disciples to pray, after acknowledging the will of His Father, He began His prayer with a plea for daily bread (see Matthew 6:9–13).

You will recall that the children of Israel, being led by Moses away from captivity in Egypt, complained: "Would to God we had died by the hand of the Lord in the land of Egypt, . . . when we did eat bread to the full; for ye have brought us forth into this wilderness, to kill this whole assembly with hunger" (Exodus 16:3).

And then we learn that manna (literally, "what is it?") was not just intended to provide food but calculated to test the willingness of the people of God to live daily in His light: "Then said the Lord unto Moses, Behold, I will rain bread from heaven for you; and the people shall go out and gather a certain rate every day, *that I may prove them, whether they will walk in my law, or no*" (Exodus 16:4; emphasis added).

In the Sermon on the Mount, Jesus taught all His disciples: "Take therefore no thought for the morrow: for the morrow shall take thought for the things of itself. Sufficient unto the day is the evil thereof" (Matthew 6:34).

When the Lord said, "Remember the worth of souls is great in the sight of God" (Doctrine and Covenants 18:10), I believe

He meant *today,* not just in some distant future place and time. Leo Tolstoy observed, "Remember then: there is only one time that is important—Now! It is the most important time because it is the only time when we have any power."

The Book of Mormon prophet Jacob spoke of a people who "because of their blindness, which blindness came by looking beyond the mark, they must needs fall" (Jacob 4:14). Our faith in Christ, our expanding knowledge of Him, occurs one day at a time, when we are fully present—not looking backward in wasted regret after repentance, not looking forward, "beyond the mark," but walking today with hope.

As I have earlier noted, about six months after I was born, my mother was diagnosed with an advanced case of cancer. The surgery was pioneering for its time, but quite radical in terms of the tissue, muscle, and glands that were removed, and immediately following the surgery my mother nearly died. As difficult as the surgery was, though, what followed was, for her, even more challenging: dozens of painful radiation treatments in what would now be considered rather primitive medical conditions. She recalls that her mother taught her something during that time that has helped her ever since:

"I was so sick and weak, and I said to her one day, 'Oh, Mother, I can't stand having 16 more of those treatments.'

"She said, 'Can you go today?'

"'Yes.'

"'Well, honey, that's all you have to do today.'"

Writing of this experience later, my mother said, "It has helped me many times when I remember to take one day or one thing at a time."

I have learned that the process of providing daily bread was not limited to the time of Moses, but that it is a way the Lord consistently teaches us to trust Him, to seek His strength, to wait upon Him. That is how we learn faith, or rather how we learn to use our faith.

Living in the present, seeking sustenance sufficient for this day, means neither simply drifting nor expecting that each day we will improve our performance over the prior day: the former lacks virtue; the latter lacks reality. Rather, a focus on the opportunities of a single day teaches us to build our trust in the enabling power of the Atonement of Jesus Christ and tutors us in the character of the Savior. I recently heard someone say that in Latin the words for *faith* and *loyalty* are closely related, and that connection resonates with me: I express my faith by being loyal to Heavenly Father and to His Son. And that loyalty is tested and finds expression each day. It is the same lesson the people of Lehi learned through use of the Liahona, as Alma taught his son Helaman:

> And [the Liahona] did work for them according to their faith in God; therefore, if they had faith to believe that God could cause that those spindles should point the way they should go, behold, it was done; therefore they had this miracle, and also many other miracles wrought by the power of God, day by day. . . .
>
> And now, my son, I would that ye should understand that these things are not without a shadow; for as our fathers were slothful to give heed to this compass . . . they did not prosper; even so it is with things which are spiritual.
>
> For behold, it is as easy to give heed to the word of Christ, which will point to you a straight course to eternal bliss, as it was for our fathers to give heed to this

compass, which would point unto them a straight course to the promised land. . . .

O my son, do not let us be slothful because of the easiness of the way; for so was it with our fathers; for so was it prepared for them, that if they would look they might live; even so it is with us. The way is prepared, and if we will look we may live forever. (Alma 37:40, 43–44, 46)

Daily loyalty means being fully committed, holding nothing back. As we live in the present, as we are loyal to God and to our Savior, we can be filled with hope. This hope is not solely for what might happen in a distant future, but for what the Lord can do with our lives, can do with us, today.

As more and more young men and women are able to name the feelings that impel them to a specific other, or to seek congruity with their inward feelings and outward manifestations of gender, the emerging sense of self may take place a decade or more before a decision would need to be made about the direction of their lives. In other words, the trials and the blessings of our choices may be far ahead when we first come out.

To this group, and to their parents, may I particularly plead for you to live in the light of today rather than in the shadow of future uncertainties. One doesn't marry at age fourteen, so why must the decision about marriage take place at that moment? As Elder Neal A. Maxwell put it, "Our trusting contentment lets the Holy Ghost have precious time in which to do His special work." At any age, we can live in the present, allowing space for what the Lord can do with the talents and abilities our heavenly heritage has granted. Day by day we can learn the language of the Spirit, we can gain experience in identifying promptings, we can increase in faith and wisdom. We can seek grace, the enabling power made possible by the Savior's Atonement, to expand our strength and augment our righteous desires. Eventually the day of decision will come, and, having learned to trust the reality of daily bread, we will be as well equipped as possible to identify and pursue our best course.

To parents particularly, you who feel the sting of injustice in the lives of your gay and transgender children even more sharply than we do ourselves, I gratefully salute your loyalty, your love, and your desire to protect your children from unkindness and pain. I recognize that not being able to provide answers to your children is a far more difficult experience than prolonged pleading in your own prayers. No parents want to imagine their child being alone throughout his or her life. This journey will test your faith as never before. It will test your loyalty to Christ and His gospel and give you occasions to see both the shortcomings and the strengths of our lay ministry. And yet, you are the adults here. You are the ones who have had the time and experience to understand the counsel of Elder Maxwell: "Just as the capacity to defer gratification is a sign of real maturity, likewise the willingness to wait for deferred explanation is a sign of real faith and of trust spread over time." As you seek guidance from our Heavenly Father in your stewardship of your children—who are and were first His children—you will set a path for generations to come. With His help, you are equal to the challenges that will face you. I pray that your experience will be similar to that of the mother who said to me, "There's nothing I wouldn't have given if my child could have avoided all the struggles and pain that have come with being transgender, but for myself I wouldn't trade a minute because the spiritual experiences I have had have changed my life."

For bishops and youth leaders, as young people come out at

earlier ages, the need for moving beyond our own comfort zones is acute. May I speak frankly again about the use of terms? When someone identifies themselves as gay, it does not mean they are violating the law of chastity. When someone identifies as same-sex attracted, it does not mean they are chaste. The terms in and of themselves don't answer those questions, so as leaders, please do not assume—if you have a need to know, ask. Meanwhile, without *any* need to ask, you can be absolutely certain that as young people face a new understanding of themselves, they need to know there is a place for them in this Church, and that their families and Church leaders who loved them yesterday will still embrace them with empathy and acceptance tomorrow.

As we consider what the Lord desires that we will learn in this life, "we see through a glass, darkly" and "now [we] know in part." (1 Corinthians 13:12). It is misleading to assume all difficulties come from the Lord, especially when I know many of my challenges are the foreseeable result of my own poor choices. And looking around to see how our brothers and sisters are engaging with their own obstacles—comparing crosses, as it were—is exceptionally unhelpful, as if we expected God to grade on a curve. It may be more useful and more accurate to think of trials, and of the process of living for daily bread, not as tests but as revelation. Our trials can be seen as encounters that reveal us to ourselves and, much more important, as occasions when the Savior is revealed to us.

As the Apostle Paul noted, "Now, discipline always seems painful rather than pleasant at the time, but later it yields the peaceful fruit of righteousness to those who have been trained by it" (*New Oxford Bible,* Hebrews 12:11–12).

Witnessing the final months of my sweet father's life, I frequently wished and prayed that I could ease the burdens of pain, of decreased mobility, of dwindling energy, of boredom and loneliness, of no longer feeling needed. I came to learn that what must be endured is as broad as it is deep (see 2 Nephi 31:16; 3 Nephi 15:9; Doctrine and Covenants 18:22). Only through our Redeemer can we understand the purpose of pain and the point of stumbling blocks, the design of desire and the essential plan of justification and sanctification (see Doctrine and Covenants 20:30–31; 88:6; Moses 6:59–60).

I wonder if there is a relationship between our level of conversion and the extent of our experience with grace, the gift of His Atonement. If so, then an award of learning, a gift of tribulation, comes from putting us into a position where our own strength is insufficient and we are compelled to rely upon the Lord and on His grace.

Through the amalgamation of many days of walking by faith, in darkness and in light, I have also come to believe that being gay is one of the great blessings of my life. Had my existence been otherwise, it might have been easy for me to go along in the Church, with the testimony I had, and to have had a happy and relatively problem-free life. Because I am gay, there came a time when I had to *know,* not merely believe, that Jesus Christ lives, that I will be resurrected as He was, and that through the power of His Atonement I can gain strength and power to become His worthy disciple. I know in the same way that Peter knew, for flesh and blood have not revealed this unto me, but our Father which is in heaven (see Matthew 16:17). And with all the love in my heart and with all the power and integrity my soul can muster, to Him I acknowledge, "Thou art the Christ, the [living] Son of the living God" (Matthew 16:16).

I am grateful that, like Paul with his thorn in the flesh that

37

God did not remove (2 Corinthians 12:7–8), the Lord has shown me His strength by allowing me to be me, and yet through His sufficient grace provided a path to come to know Him. With the prophet Joshua, I have experienced the Lord's promise: "As I was with Moses, so I will be with thee: I will not fail thee, nor forsake thee" (Joshua 1:5).

I do not have all the answers I would desire about the plan of salvation and my place in it. Like Nephi, I do not know the meaning of all things, nevertheless, "I know that he loveth his children" (1 Nephi 11:17). I do know that all answers will eventually be forthcoming, through direct revelation and through prophets, but perhaps only in the eternities. "When you climb up a ladder," said Joseph Smith, "you must begin at the bottom, and ascend step by step, until you arrive at the top; and so it is with the principles of the gospel—you must begin with the first, and go on until you learn all the principles of exaltation. But it will be a great while after you have passed through the veil before you will have learned them. It is not all to be comprehended in this world; it will be a great work to learn our salvation and exaltation even beyond the grave."

I think what Joseph was teaching us is that in the eternities we may need the loyalty and faith we have developed on earth through our experience of learning to trust daily bread. While the method of counting minutes and hours in the next life may be different from what we now know, the process of patient perseverance and learning day by day may be the same.

A few months ago, I was staying with family members and observed an interaction that has remained with me. A near-teenage child of the family, a really wonderful young person, kind, joyful, a peacemaker, had neglected to turn in some assignments at school. Although this child was smart and able to earn high grades, the forgetfulness seemed to have become something of a pattern, with a devoted and attentive mother reminding and cajoling while becoming increasingly frustrated. A much-anticipated family activity was on the horizon, and the parents had to tell their child his participation was at risk because of the failure to perform according to his abilities in school.

The next morning the youngest child, in family prayer before leaving for school, earnestly and tenderly pleaded with Heavenly Father that the older sibling would be able to join the family activity. Unknown to the youngest, the parents had already decided that not including their older child would be a punishment for the whole family and therefore not an effective way to deal with the situation.

As I talked with the parents, they expressed their sorrow at having to withhold any good thing from their child; they spoke of wanting to reward him for doing that which was required, of which he was fully capable. The three of us shared heartache that this wonderful, beloved child was struggling to learn lessons that, while straightforward, would be nonetheless essential to his ability to make the most of the gifts and talents he possessed.

As related in the seventh chapter of the book of Moses, the Lord showed Enoch the generations of the world, and we read "that the God of heaven looked upon the residue of the people, and he wept" (Moses 7:28).

It struck me, while watching my beloved family members struggle with how to help their child grow and become all of which he is capable, that this was a type and a shadow of the experience of our Heavenly Parents. Their hearts, I believe, burst with the desire that each of Their children should receive every possible blessing; as Christ said, "all that my Father hath"

(Doctrine and Covenants 84:38). I believe They weep as They watch me and you when our actions (or inactions) impede their ability to convey all that would be for our good. Perhaps we lack the vision to grasp how every commandment reflects Their love, and thus we repeatedly fail to fully live our love for Them.

I think of our Savior and Redeemer in Gethsemane. In His words, His "suffering caused myself, even God, the greatest of all, to tremble because of pain, and to bleed at every pore, and to suffer both body and spirit—and would that I might not drink the bitter cup, and shrink—Nevertheless, glory be to the Father, and I partook and finished my preparations unto the children of men" (Doctrine and Covenants 19:18–19). How can I possibly negate and refuse this most precious gift, the greatest love offering ever given?

> *What praises can we offer*
> *To thank thee, Lord most high?*
> *In our place thou didst suffer;*
> *In our place thou didst die,*
> *By heaven's plan appointed,*
> *To ransom us, our King.*
> *O Jesus, the anointed,*
> *To thee our love we bring!*

I know that grace is real. I humbly acknowledge the generosity of our Savior, as well as His endless loving patience. As we understand from Zenos's allegory of the vineyard (see Jacob 5), the Lord will make every possible effort to reach and to save His children. Only in hindsight have I been able to see the path that has been created for me as I have walked day by day with imperfect understanding but with hope and loyalty, stumbling and getting up again. It is a path where faith has grown, where belief has become knowledge, a path for which my gratitude is boundless. I know firsthand the goodness of our God, and I know it is not limited to me. I know He provides daily bread if we will but wait upon Him and accept what He offers. I pray that each of us, in our gratitude for His superlative gift to us, will also reflect on the impact our lives have on those who follow us. I pray that our actions, our commitment to daily loyalty to our Father and to our Savior, will provide fertile soil of faith for those who are only now beginning to consider the longings of their hearts.

CHAPTER 5

Times and Seasons

There's a wideness in God's mercy like the wideness of the sea;
There's a kindness in his justice that is more than liberty.
There is welcome for the sinner and more graces for the good;
There is mercy with the Savior; there is healing in his blood.
For the love of God is broader than the measure of the mind;
And the heart of the Eternal is most wonderfully kind.
If our love were but more faithful, we should take him at his word,
And our life would be thanksgiving for the goodness of the Lord.

—FREDERICK WILLIAM FABER

You may recall a campaign a few years ago that was called "It Gets Better." After a rash of gay teenage suicides, a group in Los Angeles got together to create a video of famous people sending the message to kids that growing up gay can be horrible, but it really does get better, and life is worth living. For me, it started getting better when my family moved to Delta, Utah. There were still a couple of difficult experiences, but I recall the three years there as being filled with fun and enjoyment.

As I write this, I am imagining you reading these words. If you are a gay or transgender teenager, please believe me that it really does get better. You will find those who love you and want to be part of your life. Your Heavenly Father knows you completely, the whole of you, and loves you. He is eager to help you on your journey.

While you may deal with issues of bullying at school, by and large your generation is the most accepting, most open-minded we have seen, with an almost inborn sense of fairness and inclusion. I have wondered if it is a coincidence that this generation has appeared at the time when the Lord requires a hastening of His work. Perhaps because this generation has a particularly strong ability to love generously those who are least like them, these are the souls the Lord has saved to break down the final barriers to preaching His gospel to all the nations.

If you are the parent of an LGBTQ child who has recently come out, I also promise you that it gets better. Please start with the knowledge that there is nothing shameful about being gay, lesbian, bisexual, transgender, or queer. Our Church leaders have made it clear that there is no sin in attraction. Nothing about your child makes him or her an enemy to God. Homosexuality is simply a fact in this world, and its occurrence is somewhat more frequent than having green eyes or red hair and somewhat less frequent than being left-handed. There is nothing to hide or be embarrassed about. And the very good news is that our society is quickly coming to understand this. Please be sure your child understands that, although there are choices to be made, there is nothing intrinsically wrong or shameful about him or her. Nothing.

I wish my mother were still here to deliver this message. Unbeknownst to me at the time, apparently when some of my nephews were young teenagers at a family reunion and had just learned that I would shortly be arriving with my partner, they were sharing some laughter about gays coming to the reunion when my mother came around the corner. She was a little less than average height, on the thin side, and a rather mild person. My brother Wade was witness, though, to her righteous and powerful indignation on that occasion, which left a few boys quaking in her wake: "You will *never* speak like that again about my son!"

It gets better for parents, too. The initial shock of discovery wears off, the feeling that the world has turned upside down diminishes with time, communication gets easier, and thriving in ambiguity is a skill that can be learned and practiced.

To bishops and youth leaders who may be reading this, may I also plead with you that now is the moment to draw LGBTQ youth closer, not to push them away. I promise you that these young men and women are worthy, that identifying themselves as queer, for example, does not mean they are having sex or doing anything inappropriate. They are learning about themselves and trying to live honestly in the world. Please, please let them know that you love them, that you want to be part of their process, an ally in their daily lives. Make even greater efforts to include them in activities, in priesthood callings, in opportunities to develop their spiritual strength. Their courageous openness is a great favor to you in your stewardship: in the same way we wouldn't mix young men and young women in sleeping arrangements at campouts and treks, we wouldn't put all the gay kids in the same tent. The same is true, obviously, for mission presidents: what a help that LGBT missionaries are self-identified rather than hidden, as inspiration is sought in assigning companionships. The point is this: hanging out with straight kids all their lives hasn't turned the gay kids straight. Certainly the reverse would also be true: spending time with the gay kids is not going to make the straight kids gay. What we most need to focus on is ensuring that the gay kids come to the event, knowing that they are wanted and will not be the subject of cruelty or indifference.

I could relate heartbreaking stories about the impact in the lives of young people who have been shunned by their peers or by leaders at church. Such things have no place in the Church of Jesus Christ. We may feel awkward or ill-informed, but that is no excuse for not reaching out in love to *all* those in our stewardship.

The desire to serve a mission is as appropriate and as realistic after your child comes out as it was before. In past generations, men and women often didn't come out until they were in their twenties, largely because they were doing so in a society that marginalized and demeaned them. The beneficial aspect of this timing was that many had served missions and had experiences that taught them of the Savior's Atonement. They could distinguish spiritual promptings. They had seen the Spirit at work in the lives of others. And they could bring that maturity to their decision process.

It is wonderful that there is so much more acceptance and openness now that young people can openly go through the process of learning about themselves—but it has had the unfortunate effect of causing many to decide in their preteen or early teen years that there is no place for them in the Church and they might as well drop out now. This can result in a lack of spiritual life or grounding at a time when youth most need it. Many of us are living testimony that there indeed is a place in the Church for LGBTQ people; more important, the opportunities to mature, grow, and season in the things of the Spirit are available to all, gay and straight, if they will do the work to access them and support is given to assist them in that work.

Another word to parents: as you look ahead to the choices your child will make—to be celibate, to marry someone of the same sex, to marry someone of the opposite sex—you will recognize that there is a substantial cost to any choice. It is so much easier to bear pain or suffer yourself than to see your child do so. It is in the nature of parents to want to smooth the path for their children, to ease their way.

In my own experience, after I had returned to church and begun to feel more frequently the witness of the Spirit, there came a time when I felt there was an absolute, fundamental question for which I needed to gain an answer: is it possible for a wholly just, perfectly merciful, completely loving God to allow the earth experience to require significant sacrifices and even suffering for some of His children of a kind and magnitude not placed before others?

I felt there were questions that would follow on from that answer, but I had to gain a personal witness that Heavenly Parents would ask that I subjugate the deepest yearnings of my heart: to love and be loved by a unique other. As I looked at the roughly 94 percent of the world around me of straight people, I could not see that there was any similar requirement of them. They were free to pursue the joys found in following their hearts. They could experience the first flush of falling in love, not in secret but with the approbation of those who cared for their happiness. They could marry, discover the difficulties and delights of learning to put the needs of their spouse ahead of their own, and do so with the active and visible support of the community around them. They could have and raise children (again learning the lessons of sacrifice), help those children develop and grow, teach them the gospel, and all the while be assisted and sustained by a congregation, a neighborhood, and an extended family.

As Latter-day Saints, our sense of the purpose of this life is bound up in these lessons: self-sacrifice, putting the happiness of another first, learning to lovingly guide while respecting the intellect and agency of those in our stewardship. Seemingly, the laboratory best equipped to provide education in such lessons for the eternities is a family. Certainly that is the experience of most of our brothers and sisters in this life. And yet, going back to that fundamental question, would my Heavenly Parents require that I not follow the hunger of my heart, the desire that felt like it was encoded in my DNA, to make the relationship with my partner of nearly two decades a holy place to be continually tutored in the knowledge of heaven through the experience of earthly love?

The process of gaining an answer to that question was a prolonged one for me, a matter of concerted study and prayer over a period of years. The answer, when it came, provided strength to move forward in a manner reminiscent of the experience of Enos:

> Knowing my father that he was a just man—for he taught me in his language, and also in the nurture and admonition of the Lord—and blessed be the name of my God for it—
>
> And I will tell you of the wrestle which I had before God . . .
>
> . . . my soul hungered; and I kneeled down before my Maker, and I cried unto him in mighty prayer and supplication for mine own soul; and all the day long did I cry unto him; yea, and when the night came I did still raise my voice high that it reached the heavens.
>
> And there came a voice unto me . . . (Enos 1:1–2, 4–5)

If this, the very basic question for which I needed to gain a response in order to move forward, is also a question that resonates with you or with those you love, don't be afraid to ask Heavenly Father about it. It is not my place to answer the question for you; that is a personal witness for you to gain. There may be other questions that are fundamental to your ability to determine your path. As you ponder the question, though, you might consider some examples we find of God's dealings with His people in the past.

In the book of Alma we read of the suffering of innocent people, which the Lord's prophet was constrained from stopping in order that the purposes of the Lord might be fulfilled. You will recall that many of the citizens of the city of Ammonihah had hardened their hearts against Alma and Amulek's teaching about the coming Messiah, the power of His Atonement, the judgment, and the Resurrection. Their anger was so fierce that Alma and Amulek were smitten and imprisoned, the believing men of the city were stoned and cast out, and women, children, and scriptures were thrown into a fire. "And when Amulek saw the pains of the women and children who were consuming in the fire, he also was pained; and he said unto Alma: How can we witness this awful scene? Therefore let us stretch forth our hands, and exercise the power of God which is in us, and save them from the flames. But Alma said unto him: The Spirit constraineth me that I must not stretch forth mine hand" (Alma 14:10–11). The Lord did not save His faithful followers from terrible suffering in that instance.

Jeremiah is sometimes called "the weeping prophet"—and he was depicted that way by Michelangelo in his stunning mural on the ceiling of the Sistine Chapel—perhaps because the fall of

Jerusalem and the destruction of Solomon's temple occurred as a result of the people's failure to heed his warnings. Jeremiah is considered by the Jews to be the second greatest prophet, in light of his role in teaching the people of the tribes of Israel and being the Lord's mouthpiece in some of His greatest promises concerning the last days:

> And they shall be my people, and I will be their God:
>
> And I will give them one heart, and one way, that they may fear me for ever, for the good of them, and of their children after them:
>
> And I will make an everlasting covenant with them, that I will not turn away from them, to do them good; but I will put my fear in their hearts, that they shall not depart from me.
>
> Yea, I will rejoice over them to do them good, and I will plant them in this land assuredly with my whole heart and with my whole soul. (Jeremiah 32:38–41)

Jeremiah also received a personal injunction from the Lord: "Thou shalt not take thee a wife, neither shalt thou have sons or daughters in this place" (Jeremiah 16:2). It is not apparent whether the proscription on marriage and family was ever lifted for Jeremiah in another place and time in his life. This passage indicates that some faithful people have unique circumstances in regards to life, marriage, and family.

Similarly, early faithful Latter-day Saints endured extreme circumstances or deprivation to enable the creation of a new community, Zion, that embraced people who were rejected for their identity, beliefs, or practices, including their marriage practices.

Our Mormon pioneer ancestors came to know God and create their vision of Zion through severe trials, sacrifices, and suffering.

My own Warnick ancestors, who were converted to the gospel of Jesus Christ in 1860 in Denmark, lost the home they occupied as tenant farmers because they were now Mormons. They found other employment and saved for six years to be able to immigrate to Utah in 1866. After the ship at last arrived in New York Harbor, the company of Saints traveled by steamer to New Haven, Connecticut, then boarded a train, riding in dirty freight and cattle cars. A cholera outbreak began to take its deadly toll, and soon the Mormon company was unloading the dead and near-dead at every stop along the way in an effort to control the spread of the disease. Those still living upon arrival in Missouri were transferred to a steamboat and then joined Church teams to take them the rest of the way across the plains to Utah. Nearly two-thirds of this company died during the trek. Of the eleven Warnick family members who had undertaken the journey, only four were still living when these pioneers arrived in Utah, including my great-grandfather, then sixteen years of age.

I recognize that the suffering experienced by our pioneer forebears is not the same as an individual's challenge today who may be living without spouse and family. I cite these heartrending examples, which are notable because they are outside the norm of our lives today, to propose that we would not be the first to have large obstacles placed in our path as we attempt to follow the Lord, nor the first to experience pain and distress in that journey. Perhaps it is an indication of the Lord's faith in us that unique trials are placed in our path, a sign of His loving desire that our mortal experience will be as rich as possible.

I do not know why the Lord requires sacrifices from some of

His children that He does not require from others. But it is clear that He sometimes does so. To specifically address the challenge of applying our understanding of the law of chastity to lesbian, gay, bisexual, transgender, or queer Saints, sometimes the comparison has been made between them and other single brothers and sisters who desire marriage but for various reasons have not had that blessing. The law of chastity and its requirements are the same for each, people point out. May I suggest that there is at least one significant difference? Whereas a single straight sister can pray each morning that today will be the day she will meet the man she will marry in the house of the Lord, a gay brother striving to be celibate will pray each morning that his heart will be closed, that he will *not* meet a man whom he would desire to love and marry.

Some lesbians and gays and especially bisexuals are able to find sufficient desire and attraction to create a successful marriage with a straight, opposite-sex spouse. Even though they feel their desire to marry in this way is righteous, the challenges may be considerable for both spouses and, for some, lifelong. I have not found reliable statistics, but in my experience divorce, even after children have been born, is not uncommon and is especially painful. Sometimes called "mixed-orientation marriage," this is no panacea and should not be entered into lightly or without a great deal of prayerful consideration and possibly professional counseling. As noted, the lives of children, besides that of the straight spouse, may also be impacted.

Again, my desire here is not to answer the question about what God may ask of you. That is for you to learn for yourself.

As we struggle with this question as well as others, the prophet Isaiah had words of caution for us, that we not become people "which say to the seers, See not; and to the prophets, Prophesy not unto us right things, speak unto us smooth things, prophesy deceits" (Isaiah 30:10).

If I may address a few words to parents specifically: my sense is that you will need to find your own answer to the question of God's apparently differential requirements of His children. Only with a personal understanding of the nature of God and a knowledge of His awareness of and love for your child can you continue to move forward with faith. I pray the Lord's blessings on you as you seek answers in your parental stewardship and in your own path of discipleship.

Whatever choices your children may make, I believe a focus on the inspired words of Mormon will be a critical guide to parents and to each one of us:

> Wherefore, cleave unto charity, which is the greatest of all, for all things must fail—
>
> But charity is the pure love of Christ, and it endureth forever; and whoso is found possessed of it at the last day, it shall be well with him.
>
> Wherefore, my beloved brethren, pray unto the Father with all the energy of heart, that ye may be filled with this love, which he hath bestowed upon all who are true followers of his Son, Jesus Christ; that ye may become the sons of God; that when he shall appear we shall be like him, for we shall see him as he is; that we may have this hope; that we may be purified even as he is pure. Amen. (Moroni 7:46–48)

As Mormon wrote to Moroni, hope is a gift of the Spirit, "which Comforter filleth with hope and perfect love, which love endureth by diligence unto prayer" (Moroni 8:26). It has been my experience that the hope, love, and prayers of parents are important factors in helping establish an atmosphere in which the Spirit can do His work, in the Lord's own time, in the lives of the children in their stewardship. This will not happen in a way that abridges the children's agency, but parents can create an environment where the whisperings are more likely to be heard. While wonderful parents can set the table, as it were, each of us must decide that we want to be seated there and that we desire that which is being offered. I have been liberally blessed through the influence of such parents in my life. Through my experiences and efforts, I have come to share their hope in Jesus Christ, in His unchanging goodness, in the enabling power of His mercy. I am a witness that none are beyond the reach of His Atonement, that we may be united in our families, and that we may be one with our Redeemer and His Father.

CHAPTER 6

Condoning vs. Accepting

Know this, that ev'ry soul is free
To choose his life and what he'll be;
For this eternal truth is giv'n:
That God will force no man to heav'n.

He'll call, persuade, direct aright,
And bless with wisdom, love, and light,
In nameless ways be good and kind,
But never force the human mind.

—Author unknown

All the hardest questions of mortality invite the challenge of seeking individual revelation. Can a perfectly merciful and just God require or allow differential suffering of His children as part of their mortal learning process? Gaining an answer to that question may be the first step you as a parent will take on the path of loving and supporting an LGBTQ child. Likely the next question to arise for you will be how to balance your love and acceptance of your child with your understanding of the commandments, and in particular the law of chastity.

Elder Jeffrey R. Holland, in his usual insightful and eloquent way, observed in a recent general conference:

At the zenith of His mortal ministry, Jesus said, "Love one another, as I have loved you" (John 15:12). To make certain they understood exactly what kind of love that was, He said, "If ye love me, keep my commandments" (John 14:15) and "whosoever . . . shall break one of [the] least commandments, *and shall teach men so*, he shall be . . . the least in the kingdom of heaven" (Matthew 5:19). Christlike love is the greatest need we have on this planet in part because righteousness was always supposed to accompany it. So if love is to be our watchword, as it *must* be, then by the word of Him who is love personified, we must forsake transgression and any hint of advocacy for it in others. Jesus clearly understood what many in our modern culture seem to forget: that there is a crucial difference between the commandment to forgive sin (which He had an infinite capacity to do) and the warning against condoning it (which He never ever did even once)."

Our primary focus as we seek to follow commandments is properly as the Savior instructed: first and foremost, whole-hearted, whole-minded, whole-souled love of God our Father; and second, love of His crowning creation, our brothers and sisters. As our love of God drives us to emulate Him, so our love of every member of His family impels us to witness and to walk with them, to succor and sustain, to bear up and to bear with.

There is a saying in the transgender community: it's all about the bathroom. This implies that conceptually having some sense of the enormous challenge that gender dysphoria represents is a reach most people can make and for which they can muster compassion. (In my inadequate way of trying to understand, an analogy might be to vertigo: the feeling that you can't quite get your feet on anything solid, and every element of your being feels out of kilter.) But when the conversation turns to access to a public restroom, the well of empathy often runs dry.

And as much as we try to create understanding that being gay is so much more than sex (and for many of us, means so much more and no sex!), there are often decisions to be made about dating, about living together, about marriage—about bedrooms.

I share the example of my parents' way to handle this with some hesitation. First, of course, I wish they were here to talk about this from their own perspectives. Second, their way of dealing with the question needn't be your way, and I hope you will seek your own inspiration in leading your family. I am the youngest of my parents' five sons, and was in my thirties when this experience occurred.

The first time I brought my partner for a few days' visit to my parents' home, they had already stayed with us in our home in San Francisco. They immediately liked him (and that feeling grew to a deep love over time, on both sides) and enjoyed his quick mind, his thoughtfulness, his gentle kindness, and his dry wit. As we were flying to Salt Lake City for our visit, he asked me what sort of sleeping arrangements I thought my parents might be comfortable with. My only hope was that it wasn't going to be an awkward conversation. When we arrived at their home, Mom opened the door, gave us kisses and hugs, and said, "Why don't you take your bags to the corner room downstairs—it has the best bed and the best air conditioning." And that was that, no conversation at all. I was relieved, and my partner was grateful. And another barrier that might have been erected, that might have made us feel not quite at home in their home, vanished.

That was the practice they followed. Over the following years and decades, anything that was family related included both of us. My brothers and their wives were constantly welcoming and gracious, and my nieces and nephews dealt with having an extra uncle seemingly without much difficulty. Other families may feel inspired to follow a different path due to their own circumstances.

When my partner and I first got together, my brother Todd was a member of the First Quorum of the Seventy and later in the Presidency of the Seventy. When he would speak in conference, we would fly to Utah to be in the Conference Center during his address, to be united with my parents and siblings in our support of him. Perhaps the most public example of his graciousness was in the general conference address he gave in April 2008, after having been called as an Apostle, when he said, "In acknowledging blessings, I include my dear brothers and their spouses who, as it happens, are present today." Although my partner and I were not married, we both appreciated his deft acknowledgement of our inclusion in the family.

When my parents reached the milestone of their golden anniversary, my brothers and I talked to them about how they would like us to celebrate the event. We had a wonderful dinner and reception, held in the nearby stake center, and they were able to greet hundreds of family members and friends. But when it came time for their sixtieth anniversary celebration, they said that they would like to have a dinner with just the twelve of us (themselves and their five sons and partners). We arranged the dinner in the McCune Mansion in Salt Lake City and had a glorious evening talking and reminiscing about our experiences as a family. A family photograph taken that evening, blown up to a very large size, hung over the fireplace in their family room until after Mom's passing, and then was on the entry wall of Dad's apartment in an assisted living center. That photo of Mom, Dad, my brothers and their wives, and my partner and me had a deep impact on many who saw it. One friend of the family noticed it when he and his father, who had been a counselor to my father in a bishopric in New Jersey, were visiting. He said he learned an important lesson about a loving, loyal family just by seeing that photo displayed in such a prominent place.

Although my partner and I never married, I feel quite confident I know how my family would have dealt with that event because their desire to be fully engaged in all the important moments of my life was so consistent. If you are the parent of a gay child who decides to marry a same-sex partner, I encourage you to be there, to participate fully and with happiness for their happiness. If you decide not to participate in that important moment in your child's life, you may have many years to regret the divide that can be created. Please believe me when I say that your children know everything the Church has said on the law of chastity; your absence from a wedding ceremony will neither increase their knowledge of doctrines and policies nor decrease their estimation of your conversion and commitment to obeying commandments. But what an opportunity this can be to increase family unity, to show pure love, and to solidify relationships! Just as your children will not be in doubt about your personal discipleship, neither will they doubt the importance you place on being a lovingly engaged part of their lives.

Now, does all of what I have just related constitute condoning sin? In my view, it need not, and it certainly did not in the case of my family. I realize that there is an unending variety of family circumstances, attitudes, and personalities that influences what messages get sent and received in our interactions, so each will need to determine what is best for them. And what is best for any given family may well change over time. The need for thoughtful prayer and the inspiration of the Spirit is not likely to disappear. I have never been in any doubt about my parents' or my brothers' understanding of what prophets teach and have taught. I did not misunderstand their loving acceptance of the realities of my life as any loosening of their own firm spiritual moorings.

At a Church Educational System devotional for young adults in September of 2014, my brother said:

> In reality, the best way to help those we love—the best way to love them—is to continue to put the Savior first. If we cast ourselves adrift from the Lord out of sympathy for loved ones who are suffering or distressed, then we lose the means by which we might have helped them. If, however, we remain firmly rooted in faith in Christ, we are in a position both to receive and to offer divine help. If (or I should say when) the moment comes that a beloved family member wants desperately to turn to the only true and lasting source of help, he or she will know whom to trust as a guide and a companion. In the meantime, with the gift of the Holy Spirit to guide, we can perform a steady ministry to lessen the pain of poor choices and bind up the wounds insofar as we are permitted. Otherwise, we serve neither those we love nor ourselves.

I have used the term *acceptance* in conjunction with, and perhaps synonymously with, *love*. I mean it to convey the willingness to recognize reality. While the origins or causes of LGBTQ identity or orientation are unclear, my experience, which is broadly shared, is that this reality is not one that is changed through prayer or faith: "This son's sexual orientation did not somehow miraculously change—no one assumed it would."

Accepting others does not mean that we condone, agree with, or conform to their beliefs or choices, but simply that we allow the realities of their lives to be different from our own. Difference is not conformity; in fact, it is exactly the opposite. This is especially important for LGBTQ youth, for whom guilt or pressure to conform can be harmful or destructive as they struggle to find identity. A willingness to accept the realities of another's life conveys respect for agency, for maturity, for responsibility, for intelligence. For example, suppose we know a man, severely injured, who becomes paralyzed: do we honor his circumstances by pretending that nothing has changed, or do we reflect greater compassion when we recognize the challenges, opportunities, frustrations, and joys of his new situation? I would hope that we will not be stingy with either the word or the feeling of *acceptance* for the actuality and authenticity of the lived experiences of our LGBTQ brothers and sisters. By so doing, we do not diminish our understanding of their ability to make choices in their lives; rather, we increase the clarity of the distinction between orientation or identity and behavior.

Victor Frankl, the great Austrian psychologist who was interned by the Nazis in the Auschwitz concentration camp, drew from his own experience the critical lesson: "We needed to stop asking about the meaning of life, and instead think of ourselves as those who were being questioned by life—daily and hourly. Our answer must consist, not in talk and meditation, but in right action and in right conduct. Life ultimately means taking the responsibility to find the right answer to its problems and to fulfill the tasks which it constantly sets for each individual."

I am reminded of a family camping trip to Lake Gogebic in the Upper Peninsula of Michigan, when I was probably about ten or twelve. You may have already gathered that I am not much of a camper, and I confess I don't much care for fishing, either. We had rented a rowboat, and Dad and I went out onto the lake to fish (I think Wade and Mom had taken a canoe to explore more of the lake). Dad brought a fishing pole and paraphernalia, and I brought a book. After some time with no success, I asked (perhaps several times) if we could go back to shore. Dad, who was probably a little annoyed at having his fun cut short, agreed, and I began to row. And row and row. It took me a while to figure out that all my labor was only taking us around in a large circle. I looked at Dad, who started laughing and asked if I wanted him to pull up the anchor. I think of that experience sometimes when the right answers aren't immediately obvious to me and I am expending a lot of energy in the search. It helps me remember that I need to have drawn close to my anchor—the Lord—in order to make real progress in my life.

We provide our loving witness to the opportunity of others to find the right answers in their lives through our acceptance, our love, and our own determination to follow the counsel that has been given to us—through personal revelation, through living prophets, through holy scriptures.

As our hearts are changed to feel more deeply and consistently the love of Heavenly Father and of our Savior, we will also pray for the gift of charity, to love as They love. In that effort, we can begin in our immediate surroundings.

Speaking at the funeral of the teenaged gay son of beloved friends, I expressed my feelings and faith at an excruciatingly difficult time:

He who judges perfectly takes into account not only our actions but also our circumstances, the biology of our bodies and the chemistry of our consciousness, as well as the desires of our hearts. We cannot know in the life of another what it means to "fight a good fight . . . [to] finish [the] course . . . [to] keep [the] faith" (2 Timothy 4:7). I am content to believe that this young man did all of those things. And that his plan of salvation is tailored to what he learned here and to what he will yet learn, and how he will yet progress.

But my fight, my course, and my struggle to keep the faith are not yet over.

My resolve is to be more consistent in reaching out to the one who seems ill at ease, the one who feels he or she doesn't fit, whether that's in church or anywhere else. My resolve especially is to help my lesbian, gay, bisexual, transgender, or queer brothers and sisters know that there is a place for them in our chapels, always, and please, come sit with me. To share my knowledge that their Heavenly Father knows them completely and loves them boundlessly.

My resolve is that I might see the spark of the Divine in each person I encounter.

Too many families have experienced the devastating loss of a child to suicide. LGBTQ youth have a higher rate of suicide attempts than do heterosexual youth. While the reality is that suicide is the result of many factors, all of us—parents and family members, Young Men and Young Women leaders, bishoprics and Sunday School teachers, all members of the Church—can help reduce at least some of those factors by simply accepting LGBTQ young people for who they are and loving them. It is a matter of life and death that we do so, with urgency! The National Suicide Prevention Hotline indicates that some risk factors include depression, mental disorders, substance abuse, hopelessness, impulsive and/or aggressive tendencies, history of trauma or abuse, loss of relationships, easy access to lethal means, local clusters of suicides, and exposure to others who have taken their own lives (either in real life or through media and the Internet).

Dr. Caitlin Ryan, a professor of clinical social work at San Francisco State University, founded the Family Acceptance Project and has written with Dr. Robert A. Rees, a professor of Mormon Studies at the University of California at Berkeley and at the Graduate Theological Union, the manual *Supportive Families, Healthy Children: Helping Latter-day Saint Families with Lesbian, Gay, Bisexual & Transgender Children.* Dr. Ryan's research shows that when parents and families reject or refuse to accept the reality of their child's sexual orientation or identity, those children are more than eight times more likely to attempt suicide than LGBTQ children whose families are accepting. Young people in families with high levels of rejecting behavior are nearly six times as likely to report high levels of depression, more than three times as likely to use illegal drugs, and more than three times as likely to be at high risk for HIV and sexually transmitted disease.

I am appreciative to Dr. Ryan and Dr. Rees for their permission to include here some of the findings of The Family Acceptance Project. FAP has identified behaviors that can increase, and behaviors that can reduce, the risk of physical and mental health problems for young LGBT adults:

Some Behaviors That Increase Risk

- Hitting, slapping or physically hurting your child because of their LGBT identity
- Verbal harassment or name calling because of LGBT identity
- Excluding LGBT youth from family and family activities
- Blaming the child when they have experienced negative actions as a result of their LGBT identity
- Pressuring your child to be more (or less) masculine or feminine
- Telling your child you are ashamed at how they look or act
- Not allowing your child to speak of their LGBT identity

Some Behaviors That Reduce Risk

- Talk with and listen respectfully to your child about their LGBT identity
- Express affection when your child tells you (or you learn) that they are gay or transgender
- Support your child even when you feel uncomfortable
- Advocate for your child when he or she is mistreated
- Require that other family members respect your LGBT child
- Tell and show your children you love them unconditionally
- Welcome your child's LGBT friends in your home
- Support your child's gender expression
- Talk with church leaders and members about supporting your child and welcoming them to services and activities
- Believe your LGBT child can have a happy future

Effective loving is far more than regularly announcing our affection to our children. Effective loving helps the child feel safe, valued, and accepted. We cannot nurture effectively unless we have taken the time to discover what is important to the people we are striving to love. "For the Lord God giveth light unto the understanding; for he speaketh unto men according to their language, unto their understanding" (2 Nephi 31:3). We should follow Heavenly Father's remarkable example and customize our messages and actions of love to the language and understanding of our family members. . . . Parents do not always feel loving toward their children. But love is more than a feeling. It may be considered a commitment to act in the best interest of another person. . . . The greatest human example of gentleness and compassion for children was Jesus. . . . [He] was attentive, appreciative, tender, patient, and loving.

Following Commandments

Meanwhile, in the midst of our showing love and acceptance to our children and those around us, how do we teach about loving commandments, particularly if we sense those we care about may feel unable to observe all of them?

When I determined I could not continue to move forward in the Church, I also could not see myself living as a "gay man." I thought I would have to be, to use a current term, a "clone" in order to fit in. It came with the force of revelation to me as I moved forward that I would still be me: I didn't have to adopt the manner of dress or speech, nor the moral values, that I thought to be the norms in my new community. Upon leaving the Church, I was determined that I would hold onto every good thing that I had received in my upbringing, all aspects of becoming a truly good person. I also resolved that I would *not* be someone who, upon leaving the Church, could not leave it alone. I wanted to move forward, to discover what was ahead of me. Though I was determined not to dwell on the past, I hoped to not lose sight of the things I had learned from my family, on my mission, and in work experiences about being of service to those around me versus living only for myself.

In a similar vein, when my partner and I met, he was a volunteer with a group in Berkeley, California, that was an offshoot of the free clinic established in the sixties called the Harm Reduction Coalition. The Coalition had a particular focus on reducing the spread of the AIDS virus among the gay population and among intravenous drug users. They provided free condoms and a needle exchange program in order to facilitate their vision: that an individual may not feel in a position to completely stop using drugs or to abstain from sex, but each person could make better choices daily that would reduce his or her possibility of contracting the virus. This policy accepted the reality of people's lives even if not supporting their choices.

Sometimes, as members of the Church, we tend to have a black-and-white view: if we have any question, then it's all false; either we're all in or we're out; either we're following all of the commandments or we might as well not bother with any of them. I believe we would do better to think, like the Harm Reduction Coalition: if my circumstances are such that I feel I cannot now do everything I would like to in order to become like the Savior, at least for today there are many important things that I *can* do.

If your gay, lesbian, or bisexual loved one has decided to look for a same-sex partner, I think you might suggest trying to select someone with whom he or she can kneel in prayer each day. My experience has been that our Heavenly Father always wants to hear from us. And if you are gay and have a partner, continue your daily practice of thanking God for the many blessings you enjoy individually and together.

If you know people who have decided that their mental and physical health will be better if they take a break from church participation, you might encourage them to continue their practice of a monthly fast. And I mean that in the sense not just of skipping meals but of purposely dedicating a period of time to fasting, reflection, prayer, and making a generous donation to those in need. (There are many organizations that do much good for those in need. I would note that 100 percent of the Church's humanitarian aid funds are used for aid—no administrative costs are deducted—making it one of the most efficient ways for people's donations to make a difference in the world.) It has been said that fasting is the easiest commandment to keep, and yet its simplicity may make us forget its power. Importantly, it causes us to live outside ourselves, at least for that period of time, to sacrifice something of worth and desirable in order that someone else's difficulties may be eased. The effort of fasting reminds us that we can control our wants. It strengthens our spirits and helps us draw closer to the Lord. Approaching God in a spirit of humble charity can reduce some of the noise around us so we can better hear His counsel.

I once heard a story of a new minister of a Protestant congregation in Salt Lake City. Apparently this minister was concerned that so many of his parishioners smoked, and he suggested that perhaps the church should offer some sort of group program in cessation counseling. He was told, "No, we can't stop smoking; that's how people know we're not Mormons."

Whether that anecdote ever actually occurred or not, it does illustrate a common tendency of those who feel that they need to disaffiliate from the Church. Sometimes they search for ways to show "I'm not one of them," discarding health practices or standards of morality. If reading this book is your last stop before throwing in your towel, I appeal to you: if you feel the need to show you are different from Mormons, then please be a more consistent Christian than we sometimes are. Be a more undeviating source of compassionate understanding. Be less involved with the distractions of the world. Your efforts to be different will make the world a better place for all of us!

CHAPTER 7

The Policy and Beyond

"Hope" is the thing with feathers—
That perches in the soul—
And sings the tune without the words—
And never stops—at all—
And sweetest—in the Gale—is heard—
And sore must be the storm—
That could abash the little Bird
That kept so many warm—
I've heard it in the chillest land—
And on the strangest Sea—
Yet, never, in Extremity,
It asked a crumb—of Me.

—EMILY DICKINSON

On November 5, 2015, I was in California on business, and during my last meeting my phone vibrated nearly constantly, indicating a considerable number of incoming messages. As I was being driven back to the airport, I saw that many messages were asking whether the reports rapidly spreading across social media about a new Church policy were accurate. That policy included for the first time gay marriage as one of the cases for Church discipline under the heading of apostasy, indicating that the children of gay unions could not receive any ordinances until their eighteenth birthdays, and then, only upon condition of renouncing same-sex marriage. I was certain these were only rumors, and I texted my brother Todd to check. His reply indicated that indeed a new policy had been released, and the copies of it online were accurate. I was stunned. I think many people were.

While apparently the policy's coverage of children of a gay union was borrowed from an existing policy covering the children of a polygamous union, I doubt that very many people at that point were familiar with those provisions. As painful as the concept was of adults I loved being labeled apostates—my conception of apostasy at that point was of an active effort to dissuade others from their faith—the thought that somehow the actions of parents would have bearing on our willingness to offer ordinances to children seemed to me completely at odds with basic gospel concepts.

I could not wrap my mind around it. As I boarded a flight to return to my home in Salt Lake City, the thought came to me that I should spend the flight delving into the scriptures to see if any peace could be found. I turned to a favorite chapter in the New Testament, the sixth chapter of John's gospel. It begins with Jesus feeding the five thousand; then at evening His disciples without Jesus went to the Sea of Galilee, on which there were high winds, and rowed out some distance. They saw Christ walking on the water toward them and were afraid. At Capernaum the next day, the Savior taught the people that He was the bread of life, telling them, "This is that bread which came down from heaven: not as your fathers did eat manna, and are dead: he that eateth of this bread shall live for ever" (John 6:58). Many of those who followed him said, "This is an hard saying; who can hear it?" (v. 59), and "from that time many of his disciples went back, and walked no more with him" (v. 66). And then this glorious passage:

"Then said Jesus unto the twelve, Will ye also go away?

"Then Simon Peter answered him, Lord, to whom shall we go? thou hast the words of eternal life.

"And we believe and are sure that thou art that Christ, the Son of the living God" (vv. 67–69).

In times past when I had read those verses, I had heard in my mind a ringing declaration of faith, of Peter's certainty. This night as I read them, the message seemed to be that when we are presented with hard things, things we do not understand, we are left with Peter to cling to what we do know: that Jesus is the Christ, the Son of the Living God.

The next evening, I was attending a concert by the Utah Symphony, a powerful performance of Mahler's Fifth Symphony. It is a long work; a performance will last over an hour. After its premiere, the composer is reported to have said, "Nobody understood it. I wish I could conduct the first performance fifty years after my death." I had a similar feeling about the policy: I wished I could fast-forward fifty years and be able to see and understand the impact of the policy with the benefit of hindsight.

At the interval, I saw that Todd had tried to reach me. I returned his call, and he said that he had just taped an interview with the managing director of Church Public Affairs, Michael Otterson. He then said, "If you feel you need to distance yourself from me, I will understand." I replied, "You have never distanced yourself from me, and I'm sure it hasn't always been comfortable for you; of course I am not going to back away from you in any way."

Time has passed, and the initial outcry has diminished, but

the policy has caused some number of people, good people, to feel that there is no place for them in the Church. Some couples I know who were raising their children in the Church, or planned to, have not wanted to put their kids into a position such as President Howard W. Hunter experienced:

> Howard W. Hunter was raised by an active Latter-day Saint mother and a good father who was not then affiliated with any church. His father did not object to the family's participation in the Church—he even attended sacrament meetings with them occasionally—but he did not want his children to be baptized when they were 8 years old. He felt that they should not make that decision until they were older. When Howard turned 12, he could not receive the Aaronic Priesthood and be ordained a deacon because he had not been baptized. Even though he was able to participate with the young men in other activities, Howard was deeply disappointed that he could not pass the sacrament with them.
>
> "I sat in sacrament meetings with the other boys," he recalled. "When it was time for them to pass the sacrament, I would slump down in my seat. I felt so left out. I wanted to pass the sacrament, but couldn't because I had not been baptized."

Some members of the Church were able immediately to feel that the policy was appropriate. Others struggled, and some continue to do so. Sometimes I have wondered if it is because we as LGBTQ Latter-day Saints are such a tiny minority in the overall population that for some it seems such a stretch to have empathy, to imagine themselves, their feelings, their actions and reactions, if they were in our shoes. And yet the experience of the policy has been to bring many more Saints into an open discussion about how we can care for all of our brothers and sisters. I think this is one very positive outcome and can have long-lasting effects.

As I have wrestled with understanding, I have reviewed one place in scripture where we are given to understand the seriousness with which the Lord looks upon sexual sin, in the book of Alma:

> For thou didst not give so much heed unto my words as did thy brother, among the people of the Zoramites. Now this is what I have against thee; thou didst go on unto boasting in thy strength and thy wisdom.
>
> And this is not all, my son. Thou didst do that which was grievous unto me; for thou didst forsake the ministry, and did go over into the land of Siron among the borders of the Lamanites, after the harlot Isabel.
>
> Yea, she did steal away the hearts of many; but this was no excuse for thee, my son. Thou shouldst have tended to the ministry wherewith thou wast entrusted.
>
> Know ye not, my son, that these things are an abomination in the sight of the Lord; yea, most abominable above all sins save it be the shedding of innocent blood or denying the Holy Ghost? (Alma 39:2–5)

In this circumstance, it is clear that this was a sexual relationship between a man and a woman. And yet, somehow, it seems that in our cultural understanding sex between men or between women is seen as more serious. Try as I might, I can't find scriptural evidence for that view, nor as far as I have found has a modern-day prophet identified additional revelation on this subject. And really, is there any value in trying to stratify degrees of immorality?

There is so much about the life after this one that we are unable to comprehend. My sense is that we are inclined to fill in many of the missing or hazy elements by extrapolating our earthly experiences and projecting them forward to the life eternal. For example, what do we really know of the association that will take place there between ourselves and others? I love hearing young children sing, "I always want to be with my own family," and yet I wonder how we will comprehend who makes up our family there, except the whole of the family of God? I doubt a celestial mansion has a dining room where each Sunday evening (are there Sundays there?), today's nuclear family—my mother and father, my brothers and I—sit around and enjoy catching up on the events of the week, since my parents are themselves the children, grandchildren and great-grandchildren of other parents, and my brothers' children, grandchildren, and great-grandchildren each have their own families. Do we fully understand the meaning of the sealing chain, extending to all before us as well as to all after us, and what that will mean for our engagement with them? Or, to consider another example, is the process for creating spirits from intelligences similar to what we know of clothing spirits in bodies, or perhaps is that process more closely aligned to how unorganized matter may be formed into worlds? (As a much-loved friend once said, "It won't be heaven to me if I have to be pregnant forever!")

I raise these questions because I am often asked whether I think I will be gay in the next life. As I extrapolate and project the experiences of this life, it seems to me that many of the attributes that make me *me* are associated in my mind with being gay, and yet, without being able to grasp the nature of relationships in an eternal realm, how can I even know if the concept of being gay the way I understand it today would have any meaning? Recognizing how little I know of what lies ahead, I am content to rely on what I do know: I know the Lord cannot lie, and He has promised all the Father has to those who faithfully seek Him. In the meantime, I take comfort from the ninth article of faith: "We believe all that God has revealed, all that He does now reveal, and we believe that He will yet reveal many great and important things pertaining to the Kingdom of God."

Elder Robert D. Hales has written:

> As we grow in the gospel, it is natural to have questions and sometimes even doubts. Genuine questions can actually fuel our spiritual growth. As we study and seek answers, doubts about matters of religion that arise from a lack of knowledge can be constructively resolved.
>
> We might ask, How do we question without becoming suspicious and losing our desire to believe? At various times in our lives, questions arise on policies, procedures, and even principles. Our attitude, or how we ask the question, is vitally important. If we demand an answer on our terms, we may not see the answer the Lord is providing for us. Or if we have strong feelings about a matter and become unwilling to listen, we may not understand the answer when it is given. To receive answers to our genuine questions, seeking with a humble heart and an open mind is the first step. Then, sincere study and prayer and counseling with priesthood leaders give us opportunities to increase in understanding. As we do, our faith grows, our testimony is strengthened, and our

doubts begin to flee away. . . . Heavenly Father . . . wants to help us grow. Therefore, He allows us to be engaged in seeking answers for ourselves.

Elder Hales concludes, "My personal experience is that answers to our prayers often come slowly over an extended period of time. As we act upon the feelings of our hearts, feelings of peace, comfort, and confirmation grow within us, and we know that we are on the right course."

Like Adam and Eve, we have the gift of choice: "thou mayest choose for thyself, for it is given unto thee" (Moses 3:17); like them, we may also be faced with difficult choices without clear understanding of how best to fulfill the purposes of our lives.

Some suggest that a mixed-orientation marriage (in which one partner is gay or bi, the other straight; one is male, the other female) is an invalid choice. Certainly great care should be taken to ensure both parties are as aware as possible of the likely challenges ahead. They must understand that the straight spouse cannot "save" the gay one, and the gay spouse cannot expect that his or her current desires will disappear, nor that a desire comparable to what straight people experience will suddenly be present. But for some people, this may be the option that works best.

Some suggest that celibacy is not only unnatural but an illegitimate choice, being against the desires of our hearts and the central learning of this life: to love someone else more than self. Elder David A. Bednar has said:

The precise nature of the test of mortality, then, can be summarized in the following question: Will I respond to the inclinations of the natural man, or will I yield to the enticings of the Holy Spirit and put off the natural man and become a saint through the Atonement of Christ the Lord (see Mosiah 3:19)? That is the test. Every appetite, desire, propensity, and impulse of the natural man may be overcome by and through the Atonement of Jesus Christ. We are here on the earth to develop godlike qualities and to bridle all of the passions of the flesh.

And so, again, for some, celibacy might be the choice to which they feel called.

Finally, many condemn the choice to marry a partner of the same sex, or to pursue any outward alignment of inwardly perceived gender. People sometimes pass judgment without respecting agency and the need for all of us to follow where we feel we are being led, knowing that the consequences of our choices will rest upon us. And they may fail to recognize that any of us might be guided in new directions over time.

As I look at the path I am following in my life—including my covenant to live the law of chastity—at the same time I have hope, and I am sure, that there will be greater light and knowledge to come, that the Lord will illuminate an understanding of my place in His plan. I draw a parallel between my situation and that of the people of King Benjamin, who lived 120 years before the Savior was born. As they listened to their prophet-king, and through the power of the Spirit, they were converted to the gospel of Jesus Christ. They likely understood that Jesus embodied the higher law of the gospel, which would subsume and replace the law of Moses. And yet, for the rest of their lives, while being converted to Christ they continued to live the Mosaic law. I feel similarly, that more fulsome and more expansive ways to understand all our relationships and connections may be forthcoming, but meanwhile it is my determination to live the law I have.

While we have hope, we also strive to avoid "looking beyond the mark" (Jacob 4:14), and we endeavor "not to counsel the Lord, but to take counsel from his hand," for we know "that he counseleth in wisdom, and in justice, and in great mercy, over all his works" (Jacob 4:10).

There can be a presumption that leaders of the Church, perhaps because of their age, are somehow unaware of—or worse, uncaring about—the realities of the lives of LGBTQ members. Clearly, there are strong age-related differences in views of homosexuality and its causes, and today's young people are vastly more comfortable with their LGBTQ peers than earlier generations have been. And yet, the supposition seems to be that unless one is gay or has a child or other close relative from whom one has gained knowledge and understanding, members of the older generations cannot possibly comprehend the magnitude of the challenge.

I am absolutely certain that there is One who understands every element of my life, every difficulty, every heartbreak and time of loneliness, every feeling of being misunderstood and inaccurately judged. He also knows every hope and desire, every time of joy and peace in my life. "He descended below all things, in that he comprehended all things, that he might be in all and through all things, the light of truth" (Doctrine and Covenants 88:6). "And he will take upon him death, that he may loose the bands of death which bind his people; and he will take upon him their infirmities, that his bowels may be filled with mercy, according to the flesh, that he may know according to the flesh how to succor his people according to their infirmities" (Alma 7:12).

In my experience, it is possible for us to ask for divine instruction, to know at some level, in almost a firsthand way, the suffering of another so that we may know how to act in His stead. I had a beloved friend who endured a devastating loss, of a kind with which I had no direct experience. One evening in great frustration as I was praying, I told my Heavenly Father that I felt helpless in the face of such enormous grief to be able to support my friend, and asked that I could in some measure understand her circumstance. The answer came without words, but I felt for a moment the awful, unmeasurable loss. To me, that experience offered the tiniest glimpse into the Savior's ability through His sacred Atonement to comprehend every moment of anguish and pain in my life, and in every life.

Without claiming specific knowledge, I am certain that among the fifteen we sustain as prophets, seers, and revelators, most, if not all, have sought and received this kind of understanding of the circumstances of the lives of LGBTQ members. I am confident that their compassion is genuine and heartfelt. Obeying and teaching what they have been given as the will of the Lord in our day is part of their apostolic commission.

As members of the Church, we have been provided the opportunity and challenge in our day to likewise expand our hearts and minds, to truly love and accept our LGBTQ brothers and sisters, as well as those going through challenges to their faith, those who struggle to overcome addictions, all who feel themselves to be different in any way. I believe our earnest desires to gain the gift of charity, that we may purely love one another as the Lord loves each of us, can transform us as a people and prepare us for the greater things He would have us do as we seek to become His worthy disciples.

CHAPTER 8

Measuring Success

All paths that have been, or should be
Pass somewhere through Gethsemane.
All those who journey, soon or late,
Must pass within the garden's gate;
Must kneel alone in darkness there,
And battle with some fierce despair.
God pity those who cannot say:
"Not mine, but thine"; who only pray:
"Let this cup pass," and cannot see
The purpose in Gethsemane.

—ELLA WHEELER WILCOX

No one gets out of this life unscathed. No matter how charmed a person's life seems to be, "in the quiet heart is hidden sorrow that the eye can't see." As a lesbian, gay, bisexual, transgender, or queer individual, or as parents of an LGBTQ child, we will face challenges, and to us is given the freedom to choose whether we will let the cup pass or if we will allow the Lord to show us His purposes in our lives.

Imagine how dull a symphony would be that consisted of only one note, played repetitively. Our minds are meant to stretch, to search, to work—hard—at finding answers. When Jesus said that His "yoke is easy, and [His] burden is light," He preceded that promise with the invitation, the requirement, to "take my yoke upon you, and learn of me" (Matthew 11:29–30). We can wish for greater understanding, or we can work, study, ponder, and pray for it, with patience awaiting the Lord's time and method of enlightenment. We can focus on what we know now, what service we can offer now, what commandments we can follow now. We can seek to develop a character that is resilient, not brittle, one that can be molded through our humble willingness to be led in paths we cannot see.

On one of those summer vacation trips across the country to visit our grandparents, the seven of us were in the car—in my memory, it was a Chevrolet BelAir sedan, but it might have been a DeSoto station wagon. It always seemed that Nebraska was especially hot, as well as flat and never-ending. (My apologies to any Nebraskans reading this!) In the early 1960s, air conditioning was still relatively unusual; only about 20 percent of cars had it, ours not among them. One day on this particular trip, however, my brother Greg determined that if we kept our windows rolled up, passengers in other cars around us would *think* that we had air conditioning! I was too young to fully appreciate the situation, but family lore says that everyone gamely kept their windows up until they could bear the heat no longer. I've wondered if passengers in other cars even noticed that our windows were closed, let alone if they felt any envy for the lucky people in the car with New Jersey plates that had air conditioning—assuming they didn't notice the sweat dripping off the faces of the people in the car that was supposed to be cool!

Perhaps there are times in our lives when we think if we

project the outward impression of the ideal life, of a model family, of perfect happiness, that others will think we have it all. However, an unreal façade won't change the reality behind it. And there is more to reality than meets the eye, always more to see and learn beyond the obvious. May I share one lesson I have learned, especially in my business life?

Very early in my career, I worked for a bank in Los Angeles. I was going to law school on nights and weekends and working in the trust department full time. When colleagues would talk about what they had done over the weekend, I would share my activities but change the pronoun of the person I had done those things with from "him" to "her." It was such a painful time, trying to be someone I was not because I supposed that it would harm my career to be openly gay (and in the early 1980s I may have been right). Perhaps even more damaging was my feeling that if people really knew who I was, they would not want to associate with me.

Shame is an awful, corrosive thing. Over time, two things happened to eliminate that useless emotion for me: I trusted a few people, and then an ever-widening circle of family, friends, and business associates, and found that almost without exception my trust was well placed and the responses I received were affirming and supportive. Of even greater import, I had the experience through prayer of coming to know that my Heavenly Father knew me completely and loved me fully.

When I accepted a position with an investment bank in New York a few years later, I made a commitment to myself that if anyone asked me about my life, I would be honest and forthcoming. I wouldn't necessarily initiate those conversations, but I wouldn't run from them, either. Progressively, while in that firm, I became more and more open. Five years later, I was offered a position with one of my clients, a large asset management group head-quartered in San Francisco. In my final interview, I told the chief operating officer that I was gay and I wanted to be sure the firm would be comfortable with me being open about that before they gave me their offer. I was assured that it would not be an issue.

And finally, when my partner and I considered moving back to New York to join the firm where I would spend the next eigh-teen years, I again said to the hiring manager that I would only want to be part of a corporation that would welcome an openly gay senior officer. She immediately said that of course they would want me to take a leadership role in helping the business move the diversity agenda forward vigorously. I also learned how to be open with clients and others. My strategy was to make a com-ment at an appropriate time early in a relationship about my partner and relating something *he* had done or said. I found that this eliminated awkward conversations later when the client had assumed I had a wife or female partner.

To sum it all up, the lesson I learned is that no one will feel more comfortable with me than I am with myself. It is pointless to keep the windows of my soul rolled up if there is no openness and integrity, no air conditioning, in it. When I exude a relaxed feeling about myself, it helps others to likewise treat being gay as a very matter-of-fact part of life. I have learned that all the aspects of my life—the good, the ugly, the delightful, the grueling, the times to savor and the times to endure—all have played a part in making me who I am:

> *. . . that all*
> *The terrors, all the early miseries*
> *Regrets, vexations, lassitudes, that all*
> *The thoughts and feelings which have been*

Infus'd
Into my mind, should ever have made up
The calm existence that is mine when I
Am worthy of myself! Praise to the end!

In my final semester at BYU, I was fortunate to be selected for an internship in the Utah State Senate, and I had the chance to meet and work with Senator Frances Farley, who would become a friend and mentor.

Frances had an incisive mind, a quick sense of humor, and a sharp temper. She was progressive in all the best senses of the word, by which I mean she had a genuine concern for those having the toughest time in life and wanted to help them with programs that were smart and efficient. I joined her campaign for U.S. Congress and worked full time on it for the next year. Frances and I walked much of the district together and knocked on hundreds of doors. We had time for many conversations about the nature of politics, the political environment in Utah, and the forces that drive voting patterns. One day, as we were walking in an older neighborhood of very modest homes, we talked with a number of people who had lost their jobs in the "Reagan Recession." Some of the comments I heard in this neighborhood were, frankly, remarkable in their casual racism and bigotry. I was stunned. I was twenty-four years old and had never heard such hateful speech. I said to Frances, "These people are on the bottom rung; their lives are really hard. Why don't they seem to have any compassion for other people who are suffering?" Her answer was painful to hear, but incisive. She said, "They need to make sure that there are people beneath them so that they can feel superior, to make sure they're not what you said, 'on the bottom rung.'"

As we are making our way through the challenges life hands

us, do we reach out with compassionate understanding to those who are also walking a difficult path? Or do we feel the need to make sure that some people are on a rung below us? If we are able to see daylight at the end of a tunnel of faith challenges, do we have increased patience and more willingness to comfort those who stand in need of comfort? Or are we dismissive of the concerns we have now solved to our own satisfaction?

I think of the lyrics to a beloved hymn, "They, the Builders of the Nation," praising those whose journey was harrowing, whose courage and faith stand as a beacon to us, who overcame incredible hardships crossing the country and creating a new society while maintaining their focus outward:

> *Service ever was their watchcry;*
> *Love became their guiding star . . .*
> *Ev'ry day some burden lifted,*
> *Ev'ry day some heart to cheer,*
> *Ev'ry day some hope the brighter,*
> *Blessed, honored Pioneer!*

There is no shortage of opportunity to give love, as Sister Jean B. Bingham said in a recent women's session of general conference: "One of the most significant ways we can develop and demonstrate love for our neighbor is through being generous in our thoughts and words. Some years ago a cherished friend noted, 'The greatest form of charity may be to withhold judgment.'"

I have often described my brother Tim as a "superhero to sixth graders." He is a man of extraordinary compassion, the sort of teacher who looks for and acts on the opportunity to reach out to a young boy or girl, to help students find their talents and gifts. In his quiet and unassuming way, he is a man who changes lives. Some months ago, having recently retired from teaching, Tim was asked to substitute for a few days with a special class for children on the autism spectrum. Relating one experience, Tim said that as they went to the school cafeteria for lunch, the room was loud with the enthusiastic voices of the other children, which was disorienting and difficult for those in his class. He said one young boy cried when he was asked to sit down at the table but seemed to feel calmer when he could stand by Tim. My brother said, "So I held his hand, and he stood next to me and ate his lunch." All of us can be like Tim: we can be attentive to individuals who feel left out or overwhelmed with the circumstances of their lives. We can take the hand of a brother or sister, encourage them to stand by us, and add our strength to theirs. There are so many opportunities to act in love, to act as disciples of Jesus Christ.

And that is the most important lesson my parents and I learned: that "success" in parents' efforts is measured by the love and unity in a family, not by the church activity of each family member—personal agency plays the key role determining that. But parents can have the greatest impact by creating an environment in which every family member feels included, respected, valued, and adored. The choices family members make will determine much of what their lives become, and all that makes up *who* they become, but home can be the one place where they are secure, where they find sustenance and give solace.

That success comes when every member of the family pulls his or her own weight. A gay family member who sits back and waits for everyone else in the family to demonstrate their love, respect, and interest before he or she will do the same is missing an enormous opportunity for personal growth and development.

Because we, as LGBTQ individuals, have likely spent time processing and trying to understand our feelings before including others in the conversation, we may have the greater ability to reach out—if nothing else, to model the behavior we hope others will exhibit. Every relationship of importance in our lives is enriched when approached with the spirit of greater concern for the needs of the other person. Scorekeeping is fatal: the relationships within a family are not a zero-sum game, and there are no individual winners. Either we all win together, through increased understanding and compassion, or we all lose that growth and accompanying deepened commitment.

At a certain point in my life, when I had more free time and financial flexibility, I determined that I wanted to make a trip with each of my brothers individually to deepen our bonds of love as well as our engagement in each other's lives. Todd and Kathy and their family were living in Mexico City at the time, where he was serving as Area President. I spent a long weekend with them, and Todd and I spent a day exploring nearby Aztec ruins and some of the cultural sites in the city. Greg and I went to the Pebble Beach Concours d'Elegance for a car-filled weekend. Tim and I spent a day in San Francisco and then took a beautiful train ride over the Sierras. Wade and I had a number of opportunities, when his business travel brought him to New York and he would stay at our home, to enjoy catching up in the evenings and taking side trips in New England. A number of years ago, all my brothers decided we should have a "brothers' weekend" at least once a year. Initially, we would go to the Los Angeles Auto Show the first weekend in January. Later the show changed its dates and we started to pick a weekend when Todd had an assignment in an interesting place. We generally spend

Friday with just the five of us seeing local sights, and then on Saturday and Sunday we join the sessions of his schedule where appropriate. We have been treated with enormous graciousness by the local leaders, who are already nervous to be hosting Elder Christofferson, only to learn he has an entourage of brothers tagging along! We love our time together on those Fridays to delight in each other's company, and afterward the four of us share the privilege of sitting at the feet of an Apostle, to learn and be edified together. I wish it were possible for every member of the Church to have that intimate experience of tutelage. It is an incomparable gift.

As I close this section of the book about my family and the lessons we have together learned, may I here express my gratitude to my former partner. Respecting his privacy, I have tried to write little about him and about our relationship. He is a talented doctor, a loyal friend, a kind and thoughtful man, and he was a delightful and devoted companion. His family eagerly and immediately welcomed me into their midst. When the time came in 2013 that I was worthy and wanted to again become a member of the Church, after months of conversation, his generous desire was that I should follow whatever path I felt would be the one of greatest happiness for me. He had reason to feel that I had chosen the Church over him, and yet he was willing to support my decision despite its cost in his life. I can think of no higher tribute to pay to his selflessness and love. He no longer considers himself a Christian, and yet he is to me a splendid example of the many truly good people who surround us. They may see the world differently but are nonetheless diligently practicing Christian principles as they seek to make their part of the world a better place.

May God bless you for your determination to bear the burdens of those you love, for your willingness to wrestle with angels (see Genesis 32:24–32, especially verse 26, "I will not let thee go, except thou bless me"), for your determination to live honestly, openly, and with faith and charity for all who surround you.

PART TWO

THE

JOURNEY

FORWARD

CHAPTER 9

Tender Mercies

Brightly beams our Father's mercy
From his lighthouse evermore,
But to us he gives the keeping
Of the lights along the shore.

Let the lower lights be burning;
Send a gleam across the wave.
Some poor fainting, struggling seaman
You may rescue, you may save.

—PHILIP PAUL BLISS

I t seems obvious now, looking back, that my taking the first steps on this path would lead inexorably to this place. At the time, I just wanted to escape the astronomical taxes of New York's Westchester County. I wanted to find a home that would be close to where my partner was doing his internship and residency, so that after long duty hours, the drive home would be short. And, yes, I knew there was a ward in New Canaan, Connecticut: it had been home to a BYU roommate. While looking at homes in town, I had frequently driven by the chapel and felt its pull.

My desire to rebuild a strong spiritual foundation for my life had been growing over the years. At first it manifested itself in just the pleasure of hearing the hymns of my youth, especially those sung by the Mormon Tabernacle Choir. Attending meetings with my parents reminded me of both the sweetness of clear purpose and the goodness of the Saints. And sitting in the Conference Center during general conference sessions brought remembered doctrines and a theology that made sense to me. My partner and I had attended several churches together over the years. Many practiced an admirable and robust Christian engagement in their communities, putting into practice the Savior's admonition to seek out and serve His sheep, and yet they seemed less at ease with the unique actuality of His Atonement and Resurrection and with the idea that His love might be shown through His giving us commandments and our love shown in following them.

As we settled into a beautiful new home, I began to attend sacrament meeting periodically. I did not want to be drawn into conversations with members or leaders; I wanted only to see if I would find there what I hoped: a commitment to Christ, an understanding of His gospel put into practice in service of those in need, a community united in the desire to become like Him. Not knowing anyone, I was free to concentrate solely on what was said and what I felt. During my teenage years I had received answers to prayers about the Book of Mormon and its purpose as a second witness of Jesus Christ, and I began again to read and ponder. When I knew that I wanted to deepen these experiences, I felt a desire to know if I would be welcome—not some glossed-over version of myself, but the whole of me, being truthful about my life and experiences. I had begun to contribute fast offerings, and with one check I slipped in a note that I would like to meet with the bishop.

We sometimes speak of the "tender mercies" of the Lord

(Psalm 51:1), and this occasion was one for me. Bruce Larson, the bishop of the New Canaan Ward, had been in his position for only a few months. He was an investment banker at Goldman Sachs who, a couple of years earlier, had been asked to head their human resources department, including their diversity programs. In that role, he had come to know and respect LGBT colleagues in his firm. I told him of my background and of my desire to attend Church meetings. He immediately said that I would be welcome, as would my partner, and that he looked forward to getting to know us. Bishop Larson said that the members of his ward were seeking to become better disciples of Christ, and since in that quest all are needed and wanted, he invited me to join that effort. He asked me to bear my testimony, which was un-expected, and my expression was a halting but sincere witness of the Book of Mormon and the Restoration of the gospel. He said that he would like to talk to the ward council to let them know of our conversation, to say he had extended a warm invi-tation to me, to ensure that they would also be welcoming, and to see if they would have any additional ideas on how I might participate. When we spoke again the next week, he said that the ward council had been very receptive to his desire that my partner and I should be made to feel welcome, and he encouraged us to actively join Church meetings and activities. I asked the bishop what I should say to other members if they asked if I had a wife. He thought for a moment and then said, "Well, I don't think it's a good idea to lie at church, do you?"

In the early months, as I began to attend church more regu-larly (but still only sacrament meeting), many times I would feel out of place and uncomfortable because I didn't know anyone other than the bishopric, who made a special point of greeting me every time I walked through the door. But I keenly felt the Spirit of the Lord during meetings. After one particularly powerful fast and testimony meeting, I spent some time writing the testimony I wanted to possess, both the things I could then say with certainty and the things I aspired to know. That summer, the bishop issued a challenge to all ward members to read and study the Book of Mormon during the school vacation break. I joined in reading, and it was a powerful additional witness to me of the clarity the book gives on Christ and His gospel. My patriarchal blessing urged me to study the history of the Church, promising that I would have many opportunities to bear testimony of it. In recommencing that study after a long fallow period, I came to a greater appreciation of and love for Joseph Smith as the translator of the Book of Mormon and as a chosen prophet and instrument of the Restoration of Christ's gospel.

One Sunday morning as we were visiting, the bishop expressed the thought that other ward members managed to be there for the full three-hour block, and he thought I might have similar stamina. I knew I could attend the Gospel Doctrine class, but I asked him what I should do during the priesthood hour. Bishop Larson (looking, I think, at my gray hair) suggested I meet with the high priests.

Recently, I sent my recollections to Bishop Larson to make certain my retelling of them here would be accurate. May I share one portion of his reply?

> On the first night that we met in my home, the thing that stands out boldly in my mind was my request of you to end our first encounter with a word of prayer. I recall of our meeting that I was as surprised at how quickly and effortlessly I was prompted and inspired to make

that request, as I was to acknowledge that, of course, you are welcome in our ward family. I firmly believe that prayer, which was humble, heartfelt and full of the Spirit, strengthened both of us for the road that lay ahead. . . . I know it allowed me a glimpse into your heart and soul at the very onset of our relationship and immediately reaffirmed in my own mind that acceptance, love, friendship, and a place in the ward were there for *everyone.*

I tried to participate in as many service opportunities with the ward as I could. I saw it as the only way at that time I could be equally yoked with other members in trying to act on the Savior's commandment to feed His sheep—sometimes literally, as when we would prepare and serve meals in a homeless shelter. It also gave me an early way of coming to know some ward members.

Something occurred in that ward in the early months as I attended that made me feel more a part—and, I think, also helped other members see me as more like them. The second counselor in the bishopric and his wife, David and Rebecca Young, had their fifth child about the time I began attending the ward. Rebecca had her hands full with her particularly active fourth child, and I offered to help with the baby, whom I came to call "Sweet Baby James." As the weeks went by, and there were more opportunities to help with James at church, my friendship with the Youngs deepened. We got to the point where a couple of times in the summer, when James was too little to go with the rest of the family boating on a nearby lake, Rebecca would drop him off at my home for my partner and me to babysit. I felt like I had passed a significant hurdle of trust, and that it was sort of a seal of approval that Rebecca would commit her young son into our care. Other ward friends would occasionally invite me to help with their young children at church, which seemed to me almost a public rite of passage, becoming "one of us."

Throughout this process, I would update my parents and brothers on what I was experiencing and ask questions about what I might do to deepen my engagement. They were wonderfully supportive, and Todd, especially, made time to really listen to me and, when asked, to offer some counsel. The evening of the day that Todd had been called as an Apostle, after general priesthood meeting, all of the family members in Utah had convened at my parents' home for pizza and ice cream. Dad offered the prayer as we gathered and asked a special blessing that Todd's calling would unite us more closely as a family, that we would do all in our power to support him in being equal to the demands and requirements of being a special witness of the Savior. I have felt that profound blessings of Todd's call have been reflected in my life in both the increased desire I had to draw closer to the Lord as well as the access to Todd's tender counsel and encouragement.

Each step along the way gave me a desire to do more, to feel more, to engage more. I would have periodic conversations with Bishop Larson about additional ways that I could play my part in the ward. He had the idea of having me prepare and give an occasional lesson to the high priests group. He wondered if that would be appropriate and discussed it at some length with our stake president.

With the enthusiastic assent of our stake president, Dave Checketts, Bishop Larson invited me to prepare a lesson. I was delighted and terrified in equal measure. The brethren in that group were incredibly accomplished, both in their professional lives and in their service to the Church at every level of responsibility. I had appreciated their very practical approach to implementing the gospel to bless individuals and families, their insight into scripture, and their absolute devotion to daily discipleship. I realized there was nothing I could teach them, but I had a great desire that we could share our testimonies with each other as we explored the topic. They were gracious and supportive—and generous in their comments afterward.

The year I began to attend Gospel Doctrine, the course of study was the Book of Mormon. Our knowledgeable and inspired teacher, Brent Alvord, provided illuminating information to help us better understand Bible parallels reflected in passages of the Book of Mormon. But above all he provided an influential personal witness of its impact in his life and the experiences that had developed his testimony of its truthfulness.

I gradually came to know and love the other members of my ward—and I say "my" ward even though for most of the years I attended there I described myself as "the most active nonmember of the New Canaan Ward." I occasionally had to remember that as wonderful as it was to feel wanted and welcomed there, "no more a stranger, nor a guest," the purpose of my participation was to commune with the Spirit, to progress on my road of discipleship, and to support others on their journey. As I began to attend other meetings and to participate in service projects, I came to know other members of the ward. I met one ward member, Brian Blair, in the Kansas City airport as we were both waiting for a flight back to New York. It seems strange now, but it was a new experience for me to be in a work setting and meet a member of the Church, and soon I began a new process of "coming out" in my work life. I began, with a small group of close friends at first (just as I had when letting a widening circle of family, friends, and colleagues know that I was gay), to say that I was attending the

LDS Church, explaining the Word of Wisdom, being open about faith, about prayer, about testimony.

I have thought about how the New Canaan Ward created such a welcoming place for me, perhaps in a different way from how other wards might have reacted. One factor may have been that as a suburb of the nation's most populous city, many people in the ward worked for large companies in which respecting and celebrating diversity was an active effort. In a big city, many ward members had close colleagues who were lesbian, gay, bisexual, transgender, or queer, and had already learned to identify areas of shared interest, building relationships of acceptance and trust. Many members had lived overseas and learned to thrive in unfamiliar settings and create relationships with those who seemed, at first, very different from themselves. I think one important factor was that the ward was actively engaged in a missionary effort, and thus was attuned to identifying new faces, greeting those they didn't know, and actively reaching out in friendship. Sadly, another component was that there were some heartbreaking divorces occurring, and from that experience ward members made a conscious effort to avoid gossip and judgment. Many ward members knew my partner—Bishop Larson once said that our meetings always started late when my partner joined me because so many members of the ward rushed over to greet him. So for the first five years I attended, they might have correctly surmised that there were aspects of my life wherein I was not living all commandments, and yet I never had a feeling that anyone there viewed me with anything other than love.

I also tried to make clear through my actions that I attended meetings solely because I wanted to learn to be a more consistent disciple. I wanted to absorb the understanding and witness that other members had gained throughout their lives. I did not come in order to pursue an agenda, with a purpose of educating other members, nor did I look for opportunities in classes to enlighten my brothers and sisters on LGBTQ issues. There were certainly appropriate times in personal conversations to respond to people's questions, and many wonderful discussions happened in that manner. I hoped that the way I was living my life spoke eloquently about my desires and priorities in worshipping with the Saints.

A "bump in the road" of those early years occurred with the Church's engagement around Proposition 8 in California, the effort to reverse the state supreme court's ruling in favor of same-sex marriage equality. For my partner, this event ended any interest he had in our church and caused him to wonder if my family really loved us or if they were just very well-mannered people hiding somehow their lack of acceptance of us. Some wonderful friends in my ward made special efforts to reach out to my partner, not because they wanted to convert him, but because they wanted to know him and befriend him. Their kindness and genuine interest helped lessen some of his barriers but never quite managed to surmount them.

Two wonderful friends that we met about this time, Ben and Julie McAdams, were introduced to us by my niece Laura. Ben was a counselor in the bishopric of her ward, and he and Julie were recent graduates of the law school at Columbia University. Both were now working in law firms in New York City. We became great friends, especially because Ben had been active in politics—he later became mayor of Salt Lake County—and because he and Julie adored my partner and surrounded him with their love. They are great supporters of LGBTQ equality as well as dedicated and committed members of the Church, and they are wonderful goodwill ambassadors for the Church in the larger community. I find them to be great examples of how we can stand for what we know to be true in a way that earns the respect of others who believe differently. After Ben and Julie had moved back to Utah, he had taken a position with then-Salt Lake City Mayor Ralph Becker as his legislative liaison. In that role, Ben played an important role in crafting a nondiscrimination ordinance for the city that could find broad support across the community. That work to find common ground can be difficult and frustrating. One evening during this period, Ben shared some of his disappointment over otherwise good people who could not seem to find space in their minds and hearts for a more inclusive city. I thanked him for his great work, and we agreed that in the end, what really matters is what we believe and know about God, His prophets, and the eternal gospel of Jesus Christ. Ben and Julie are the kind of friends I can always count on to help me find solid ground in those moments when my frustrations obscure the things that are most critical.

As his time serving as bishop of the ward came to an end, Bruce Larson and his wife, Gayle, moved to Utah, and then to the assignment as Asian regional head of human resources for his firm, based in Hong Kong. A wonderful bishop was called in his place who continued the warm welcome I felt there. One Sunday I had a marvelous conversation with President Checketts, in which he shared very personal experiences that gave him gratitude for the Savior's mercy and the desire that in his position of authority he could reflect that divine characteristic to those for whom he had stewardship. That conversation, and our sharing of deep feelings about Christ and His gospel, deepened our friendship, and President Checketts offered to make time when the two of us could study the scriptures together.

Invited to pick our first topic, the Atonement of Jesus Christ, I spent time researching relevant scriptures, general conference addresses and other writings of modern prophets, and even some lines of verse. By the time we actually met on a beautiful Saturday morning in President Checketts's study, I had about fifteen or twenty pages of material that I had used to prepare myself. That began a pattern of us meeting about once a month. I felt so powerfully in those hours a spirit of love and brotherhood, as well as the enlightening power of the Holy Ghost, "for my soul delighteth in the scriptures, and my heart pondereth them" (2 Nephi 4:15). I know the demands on President Checketts's time were enormous, in his calling as well as his profession, and I was deeply touched that he was willing to create time to do as did the Nephite disciples at the time of the Savior's appearance, "they taught, and did minister one to another" (3 Nephi 26:19). Over the course of a year or more, I realized I had experienced a crash course in the doctrines of the gospel, which helped me to feel I was starting to make up for a couple of lost decades of study!

During this time, I was asked to speak to the Arizona LDS LGBT Conference. I talked to both my brother Todd and President Checketts about whether they felt this would be an appropriate thing to do, and both were supportive. Both also provided helpful comments on the speech, beginning a frequent pattern for me of seeking and receiving counsel as I tried to share my feelings about returning to Church activity. I had accepted the invitation to speak at the Arizona conference from dear friends, Jonathan and Rachel Manwaring, many months before the event. A few days before the conference, my father passed away. The most convenient time for the funeral would have been on the day of the conference, but each of my brothers was supportive of my desire to fulfill my commitment there, and we held the funeral the following Monday. My partner attended the conference with me, and I think that may have been the only time he heard me share my feelings publicly about the Church, about Christ, and about His gospel. It was an especially tender time, as I was feeling very close to my parents and sharing my journey with many of my Latter-day Saint LGBTQ brothers and sisters and their families and friends.

From those wonderful Saints in the New Canaan Ward and from ward and stake leaders, I came to learn, as Elder Neal A. Maxwell said in his final general conference address, that "as you submit your wills to God, you are giving Him the *only* thing you can *actually* give Him that is really yours to give. Don't wait too long to find the altar or to begin to place the gift of your wills upon it! No need to wait for a receipt; the Lord has His own special ways of acknowledging." Elder Maxwell continued, "I testify to you that God has known you individually, . . . for a long, long time (see Doctrine and Covenants 93:23). He has loved you for a long, long time. He not only knows the names of all the stars (see Psalm 147:4; Isaiah 40:26), He knows your [name] and all your heartaches and your joys!"

I came to learn that the process of submitting my will to His is not a one-time event, but rather an ongoing effort each day to learn the principles of the gospel by living them. According to President Harold B. Lee, "All the principles and ordinances of the gospel are in a sense but invitations to learning the gospel by the practice of its teachings." I began to learn that to pray, study, and work for the gift of charity, the gift of loving purely as

Christ loves, is to catch a glimpse of what Heavenly Father loves about each person with whom we interact. I began to learn, in the words of Elder M. Russell Ballard, "The love [of] the Savior . . . is an active love. It is not manifested through large and heroic deeds but rather through simple acts of kindness and service." I began the process of committing to act and become as the Savior desired when He said, "What manner of men [and women] ought ye to be? Verily I say unto you, even as I am" (3 Nephi 27:27).

CHAPTER 10

A Divine Mandate

In this Church there are no strangers and no outcasts.
There are only brothers and sisters.
The knowledge that we have of an Eternal Father helps us be more
    sensitive
to the brotherhood and sisterhood that should exist
among all men and women upon the earth. . . .
In this Church our wards and our quorums do not belong to us.
They belong to Jesus Christ.
Whoever enters our meetinghouses should feel at home.
The responsibility to welcome everyone has growing importance.

—GÉRALD CAUSSÉ

Last year, I traveled to Israel and Jordan to spend nearly two weeks with three of my brothers and their wives, together with our dear friends Richard and Jeni Holzapfel. During those hot summer days, we were able to see architectural and other relics of the first century AD, places and structures that Jesus may well have seen. We felt the power of sites where the Savior's life may have begun, where His atoning sacrifice may have taken place, and where His body may have been laid to rest before His Resurrection. These were glorious days, spirit-drenched, providing remarkable gifts of insight and understanding as well as a unique opportunity to spend significant time together without the normal interruptions of life.

We also visited a very modern place, Yad Vashem, the world Holocaust remembrance site in Jerusalem. It was established in 1953 as a center for research, documentation, education, and commemoration of the Nazi Holocaust of World War II, in which an estimated six million Jews were systematically murdered, as well as the Roma people (gypsies), homosexuals, and others. The strength and capacity of this site to make tangible the lives of individual victims of hate and prejudice is profound. It is a living testament to the ordinary lives of men, women, and children swept up into the horror of Nazi loathing for those they categorized as subhuman. It is a holy place of honor and memory; I doubt anyone could leave it without feeling moved.

The Hebrew words *yad vashem* mean "a place and a name": "Even unto them will I give in mine house and within my walls a place and a name [a *yad vashem*] better than of sons and of daughters: I will give them an everlasting name, that shall not be cut off" (Isaiah 56:5).

The prophet Isaiah is speaking of the everlasting covenant the Lord has made with the house of Israel, and in the next verses expands His promises to include all of His children:

> Also the sons of the stranger, that join themselves to the Lord, to serve him, and to love the name of the Lord, to be his servants, every one that keepeth the sabbath from polluting it, and taketh hold of my covenant;
>
> Even them will I bring to my holy mountain, and make them joyful in my house of prayer: their burnt offerings and their sacrifices shall be accepted upon mine

altar; for mine house shall be called an house of prayer for all people. (Isaiah 56:6–7)

Likely all of us can think of several circumstances in which the Lord provides a place and a name for those who choose to love and serve Him, preeminently, His temples. We also gain a new name when we undertake the covenant of baptism, as we are reminded during the sacramental prayer: "they are willing to take upon them the name of thy Son" (Doctrine and Covenants 20:77).

Thus, in our chapels, as we partake of the most holy ordinance offered there, all who gather may have a place and a name.

Hanging in my home in Salt Lake City is a powerful painting by artist Elspeth Young, entitled *Other Sheep Have I*. The artist has skillfully rendered a beautiful Nephite woman on her knees before the resurrected Jesus Christ as she gazes at the wounds in His feet. Each time I look at this painting, I am reminded of the Savior's invitation. After the earthquakes, the destruction of great cities, and the darkness that filled the land, the ancient Nephites looked up and beheld a "Man descending out of heaven," "and it came to pass that he stretched forth his hand and spake unto the people," testifying of himself and of the redemptive role He had played. As the people were overcome and had fallen to the earth, "the Lord spake unto them saying: Arise and come forth unto me, that ye may thrust your hands into my side, and also that ye may feel the prints of the nails in my hands and in my feet, that ye may know that I am the God of Israel, and the God of the whole earth, and have been slain for the sins of the world" (3 Nephi 11:8–9, 13–14).

Later, the Savior reiterated to the Nephites, "And ye see that I have commanded that none of you should go away, but rather have commanded that ye should come unto me, that ye might feel and see" (3 Nephi 18:25).

Like the Nephites, we also are summoned by the Lord to feel and see, and to become recipients of and participants in the gift of His atoning sacrifice.

That invitation to feel and see has been powerful in my life. On the Friday evening before October general conference in 2013, in a chapel in Salt Lake City, with my brothers, their wives, and a few Church leaders and friends looking on, I was baptized. The magnificent bishop who welcomed me so warmly to join in the voyage of discipleship with the Saints of the New Canaan Ward, Bruce Larson, performed my baptism. The stake president, Dave Checketts, who had so generously made time each month for one-on-one scripture study, conducted the meeting. My beloved eldest brother, Todd, provided a tender and sacred confirmation blessing. Each of my brothers bore their testimonies. My sister-in-law Kathy, who excels in beautiful calligraphy, had lettered a sign that we placed near a portrait of our parents: "Dear Mom and Dad, thank you for your influence in our lives." As she said, "We may not be able to see them, but we want them to see how much we love them."

The wonderful Saints who made place in their hearts and on their pews year after year never demanded that my progress or repentance be visible to them. They simply made space. They provided a warm handshake or hug and a sincere smile. They trusted that the Spirit would guide me in my journey, as He was likewise doing for them. I believe they were fulfilling a divine mandate in doing so.

When we welcome others to a chapel, we are fulfilling the individual and inward covenants we have made at baptism to take upon ourselves the name of Jesus Christ. Those covenants are manifested outwards toward others through our commitment that we shall "bear one another's burdens, that they may be light; yea, and are willing to mourn with those that mourn; yea, and comfort those that stand in need of comfort, and to stand as witnesses of God at all times and in all things, and in all places that [we] may be in, even until death" (Mosiah 18:8–9). As we strive to become worthy of being called by His name, we seek to align our hearts with His. Then we begin to comprehend that only by loving as He loves, by willingly forsaking judgments and foregoing condemnation and criticism of others, can we become His disciples and eventually His friends (see Doctrine and Covenants 84:77). Through partaking of His sacrament, we seek to obey both the first and the second great commandments (Matthew 22:37–39).

> *Now I come before the altar, off'ring up my broken heart,*
> *Seeking for the blessed gifts His Atonement can impart.*
> *Bread of Life, Living Water,*
> *Feed my soul, fill my heart.*
> *Give to me new life in Thee,*
> *And make me whole, complete and holy,*
> *Bound to Thee eternally.*
> (Annette W. Dickman)

Thus have we been commanded:

> And behold, ye shall meet together oft; and ye shall not forbid any man from coming unto you when ye shall meet together, but suffer them that they may come unto you and forbid them not;
> But ye shall pray for them, and shall not cast them

out; and if it so be that they come unto you oft ye shall pray for them unto the Father, in my name.

Therefore, hold up your light that it may shine unto the world. Behold I am the light which ye shall hold up—that which ye have seen me do. Behold ye see that I have prayed unto the Father, and ye all have witnessed.

And ye see that I have commanded that none of you should go away, but rather have commanded that ye should come unto me, that ye might feel and see; even so shall ye do unto the world; and whosoever breaketh this commandment suffereth himself to be led into temptation. (3 Nephi 18:22–25)

Could the Lord be clearer in His injunction that the meetings we hold in our chapels are meant to be a place of welcome and of love for all who enter? And could He be clearer that none—including our lesbian, gay, bisexual, transgender, or queer brothers and sisters—should be sent away? As President Dieter F. Uchtdorf observed, "The Church is a home for all to come together, regardless of the depth or the height of our testimony. I know of no sign on the doors of our meetinghouses that says, 'Your testimony must be this tall to enter.'"

In His instruction to the Nephites when He introduced the emblems of his sacrifice, the risen Lord said:

And now behold, this is the commandment which I give unto you, that ye shall not suffer any one knowingly to partake of my flesh and blood unworthily, when ye shall minister it;

For whoso eateth and drinketh my flesh and blood unworthily eateth and drinketh damnation to his soul;

therefore if ye know that a man is unworthy to eat and drink of my flesh and blood ye shall forbid him. (3 Nephi 18:28–29)

As He warned that worthiness to participate in the sacramental ordinance is essential to our well-being, He also cautioned that the same worthiness standard does not apply to attendance and participation in meetings of Saints: "Nevertheless, ye shall not cast him out from among you, but ye shall minister unto him and shall pray for him unto the Father, in my name; and if it so be that he repenteth and is baptized in my name, then shall ye receive him, and shall minister unto him of my flesh and blood" (3 Nephi 18:30). He also indicated that certain behavior, or lack of it, may cause an individual to no longer be counted a member of His Church: "But if he repent not he shall not be numbered among my people, that he may not destroy my people, for behold I know my sheep, and they are numbered" (3 Nephi 18:31).

And yet, even in these most serious circumstances, Jesus indicated that those no longer numbered among his people are always meant to find a home in our meetinghouses: "Nevertheless, ye shall not cast him out of your synagogues, or your places of worship, for unto such shall ye continue to minister; for ye know not but what they will return and repent, and come unto me with full purpose of heart, and I shall heal them; and ye shall be the means of bringing salvation unto them" (3 Nephi 18:32).

The Lord requires all of us to open wide the doors of our meetinghouses, to make a place of embracing, of fellowship and love for (as a current example) gay or lesbian married couples raising children, even if they are no longer members of the Church. And, of course, as we think about this, would we want these families to find a home anywhere other than among us?

What might cause us to hesitate to provide such fellowship? A worry that somehow a family will evidence affection? The Beloved Apostle John provides wise counsel to us:

> There is no fear in love; but perfect love casteth out fear: because fear hath torment. He that feareth is not made perfect in love.
>
> We love him, because he first loved us.
>
> If a man say, I love God, and hateth his brother, he is a liar: for he that loveth not his brother whom he hath seen, how can he love God whom he hath not seen?
>
> And this commandment have we from him, That he who loveth God love his brother also. (1 John 4:18–21)

And Elder Jeffrey R. Holland has taught:

> As surely as the rescue of those in need was the general conference theme of October 1856, so too is it the theme of this conference and last conference and the one to come next spring. It may not be blizzards and frozen-earth burials that we face this conference, but the needy are still out there—the poor and the weary, the discouraged and downhearted. . . . Take your team and wagon; load it with your love, your testimony, and a spiritual sack of flour; then drive in any direction. The Lord will lead you to those in need if you will but embrace the gospel of Jesus Christ that has been taught in this conference. Open your heart and your hand to those trapped in the twenty-first century's equivalent of Martin's Cove and Devil's Gate. In doing so we honor the Master's repeated plea on behalf of lost sheep and lost coins and lost souls.

When Nephi desired to know the meaning of the vision of the tree of life that his father had seen, he was shown the birth of the Savior, and then he understood that the tree was "the love of God, which sheddeth itself abroad in the hearts of the children of men; wherefore, it is the most desirable above all things . . . and the most joyous to the soul" (1 Nephi 11:22–23). That love needs to characterize all our interactions.

A young friend of mine came out a few years ago to his parents while in his mid-teens, and subsequently to his family and peers in school and church. He is academically accomplished and musically talented, with a quietly engaging personality. In his early exposure to other LGBTQ people, he was dismayed at how easily and quickly some seemed to have discarded their faith, as if in order to be "truly" gay, one must almost replace the person he or she had been up to that point with an entirely new being. My friend rejected this notion as simplistic and made clear his determination to integrate all of the important elements of his life, including his orientation and his faith. Members of his ward were accepting and loving when he came out to them, to a degree that was a happy surprise to my friend and his family.

However, my friend had heard many messages before he came out that created a deep impression within him that he would be loved but not fully accepted. And over time he came to feel that the messages he heard at church about LGBTQ people in general did not feel compassionate and often did not distinguish between identity and behavior, leaving him with a sense that there really was not a place for him there. Unwilling to yield the central place Christ held in his spiritual life, he began to attend a local evangelical congregation. Recently, I asked him what the beliefs of that church are about sexual activity between people of the same gender, and he told me that this denomination has the same basic doctrine as the LDS Church in that regard. When I asked what made the difference for him, why he found the new congregation to be a more comfortable place, he told me that while they believe sex between two men or two women is wrong, they hold a view that we all sin. My friend said that the members of that church and its local leaders have made it plain to him that they want him to worship with them, and they trust that my friend is doing the best he can at this point.

Without ceding doctrine, could we not reflect greater charity to every individual, couple, and family? Knowing that the "Lord cannot look upon sin with the least degree of allowance" (Doctrine and Covenants 1:31), can we still recognize that all lives are works in process, that, as President Thomas S. Monson has observed, "Life is perfect for none of us. Rather than being judgmental and critical of each other, may we have the pure love of Christ for our fellow travelers in this journey through life. May we recognize that each one is doing [his or her] best to deal with the challenges which come [their] way, and may we strive to do *our* best to help out"? As the Evangelist proclaimed, "If we say that we have no sin, we deceive ourselves, and the truth is not in us" (1 John 1:8). We believe in the power of the Holy Ghost to convert (see John 16:13; Doctrine and Covenants 5:16; 8:2; 100:8), and thus we can patiently allow for the agency of the individual and the timing of the Lord as we care for those whom we gratefully welcome to worship with us.

We can and must reach out to others in moments when they struggle with doubt, in seasons of trial when answers to prayers seem slow in coming. When someone's love for the Church collides with the reality that all of us within it are imperfect, may we have the desire to invite every wandering lamb to partake of our Savior's Atonement. Even in circumstances when we feel our abilities are unequal to our desires to heal the wounds of another, we can quietly reach out in kindness and empathy, being willing to simply listen and sustain. Our demonstration of love for the long haul and our absolute unwillingness to judge another can be a source of daily bread to those around us. We can dedicate ourselves to welcoming everyone who crosses the threshold of our chapels, to let no one sit alone, to ensure there is never an "in group" and therefore some left out. We can pray constantly for guidance as to how we might ease the burdens of the poor in spirit as well as the poor as to the things of this world. Our efforts, along with those of faithful parents who may be unable in this life to see the end result of their virtuous influence, will be met with the Savior's sweet sustaining words: "Inasmuch as ye have done it unto one of the least of these my brethren, ye have done it unto me" (Matthew 25:40).

Our transgender brothers and sisters have perhaps the hardest challenges placed before them, and the need for accommodation from all of us around them is also greater. Our opportunity to act in love, even when we lack full understanding, can be a blessing in their lives and a unifying force in a congregation.

I pray that in our efforts at outreach, as we strive through "persuasion, by long-suffering, by gentleness and meekness, and by love unfeigned; by kindness, and pure knowledge" (Doctrine and Covenants 121:41–42), we may help all around us to find in their lives the power of the Savior's atoning sacrifice, and that through His love for all of us, we will have our "hearts knit together in unity and in love one towards another" (Mosiah 18:21).

CHAPTER 11

Growing from Grace to Grace

Pale the sky, first stars appear,
As winter light, scarce, disappears.
Keep me from the world's dark chill,
Then stir deep embers, spark Thy will.
Warm my heart, give eyes to see
Another's suffering to set free;
Christ's compassion all ablaze;
Then by His light live out my days.
Holy Wonder bind me to Thy firm,
Unshaken love anew.
So by winter's morning light,
My eyes are fresh with second sight.

—Lorene de St. Aubin

Early in my path of returning to membership in the Church, I was sitting in the quiet family room of our home in New Canaan. I was reading a general conference address, and the speaker quoted from section 20 of the Doctrine and Covenants, a revelation to Joseph Smith that provides guidance on points of both theology and organizational structure and "may have been

117

given as early as summer 1829" (section heading notes), before the Church was formally organized on April 6, 1830. These verses affirm the teachings of the Apostle John:

"And we know that justification through the grace of our Lord and Savior Jesus Christ is just and true;

"And we know also, that sanctification through the grace of our Lord and Savior Jesus Christ is just and true, to all those who love and serve God with all their mights, minds, and strength" (Doctrine and Covenants 20:30–31).

As I read those verses, the distinction between justification and sanctification was unclear to me, so I started to research the terms, and my reading led me to ponder the meaning of grace. In my mind I asked, "How could the Savior love us enough to do this?" And for a brief moment, I experienced what Joseph Smith referred to when he said revelation may come to us in the form of "pure intelligence" or knowledge, transferred in the abstract (that is, spirit to spirit) through the Holy Ghost. The glimpse I received came without words, but it brought to me an elemental understanding that our Redeemer's love is eternal, all-encompassing, and that I am included in that love, in His grace. I began to desire above all else that I might be a disciple of Jesus Christ, and that through the power of the Holy Spirit I could come to know His character, that I could come to know Him.

President Henry B. Eyring has taught:

> We can, if we live worthy of it, have the blessing of the Spirit to be with us, not only now and then, as in such remarkable experiences as [I had received that day], but always. You know from the words of the sacrament prayer how that promise is fulfilled: "O God, the Eternal Father, we ask thee in the name of thy Son, Jesus Christ,

to bless and sanctify this bread to the souls of all those who partake of it, that they may eat in remembrance of the body of thy Son, and witness unto thee, O God, the Eternal Father, that they are willing to take upon them the name of thy Son, and always remember him and keep his commandments which he has given them."

And then comes the glorious promise: *"That they may always have his Spirit to be with them"* (D&C 20:77; emphasis added).

To always have the Spirit with us is to have the guidance and direction of the Holy Ghost in our daily lives.

In sacrament meetings, in Gospel Doctrine classes, in stake conferences, in priesthood group meetings, and in my personal study, I felt the confirmation of the Spirit testifying of truth in a physical way that I had not experienced for a couple of decades.

That first conversation with Bishop Larson had taken place because I wanted to be in a place and with a group of people where I could explore the meaning and purpose of life, where I could investigate and consider the answers to the quandaries of my experiences. To the extent that I could envision a future at that point, I expected my church engagement to be additive another dimension of an already full and happy life. I did not anticipate a changed life. In retrospect, of course, I realize how naïve I was. When has the Lord ever left someone in a comfortable position, simply to go with the flow and satisfactions of his or her life? To seek to know Him is antithetical to a casual, comfortable existence. It is to engage in the inherent contradiction between eternal progress and eternal rest.

I recall an advertisement for a brand of potato chips with the slogan, "No one can eat just one!" I think our engagement with the Spirit is like that: as we begin to feel the life outside our lives, our appetite grows to make the experience deeper and more frequent. And over the course of years, the combination and culmination of minute changes becomes an entirely new direction. I did not know how my life would take shape when I began to attend the New Canaan Ward, but looking back, I can see that the path that was created for me is sharply defined and clear. My desires were changing, my priorities evolving, my goals shifting.

I thought I might share here two of the areas of focus in my conversion (or reconversion) process that might be useful to others. The first was, and continues to be, my process of gaining an understanding and appreciation of the power of the Holy Spirit. The second, also very much a journey in progress, has been my desire to understand the character of Christ.

The Power of the Holy Spirit

President Heber J. Grant described an early experience in his life:

> When I was a young man, probably seventeen or eighteen years of age[,] I heard the late Bishop Millen Atwood preach a sermon in the Thirteenth Ward. I was studying grammar at the time, and he made some grammatical errors in his talk.
>
> I wrote down his first sentence, smiled to myself, and said: "I am going to get here tonight, during the thirty minutes that Brother Atwood speaks, enough material to last me for the entire winter in my night school grammar class." We had to take to the class . . . four sentences a

week, that were not grammatically correct, together with our corrections.

I contemplated making my corrections and listening to Bishop Atwood's sermon at the same time. But I did not write anything more after that first sentence—not a word; and when Millen Atwood stopped preaching, tears were rolling down my cheeks, tears of gratitude and thanksgiving that welled up in my eyes because of the marvelous testimony which that man bore of the divine mission of Joseph Smith, the prophet of God, and of the wonderful inspiration that attended the prophet in all his labors.

Although it is now more than sixty-five years since I listened to that sermon, it is just as vivid today, and the sensations and feelings that I had are just as fixed with me as they were the day I heard it. . . . That testimony made the first profound impression that was ever made upon my heart and soul of the divine mission of the prophet. . . . This was the first testimony that had melted me to tears under the inspiration of the Spirit of God to that man.

An early insight I gained involved the desirability of certain character traits. In my business career, traits that had been held up as the most admirable included being well-spoken, polished, ambitious, charismatic, reward-driven, and knowledgeable about "the numbers." These seemed to contrast with the indications of discipleship, including humility, being teachable and willing to be chastened, a focus on individuals and service to others, resilience, charity. The personal qualities of business leaders and disciples are not mutually exclusive, but in my learning process I was reminded, as President Grant learned in the experience he related, that the accoutrements of worldly attainment are not required as the Lord seeks a willing follower. Far more crucial is the contrite spirit that allows us to seek heavenly tutoring.

Elder David A. Bednar taught this about the communications of the Spirit:

> Strong, dramatic spiritual impressions do not come to us frequently. Even as we strive to be faithful and obedient, there simply are times when the direction, assurance, and peace of the Spirit are not readily recognizable in our lives. In fact, the Book of Mormon describes faithful Lamanites who "were baptized with fire and with the Holy Ghost, and they knew it not" (3 Ne. 9:20).
>
> The influence of the Holy Ghost is described in the scriptures as "a still small voice" (1 Kgs. 19:12; see also 3 Ne. 11:3) and a "voice of perfect mildness" (Hel. 5:30). Thus, the Spirit of the Lord usually communicates with us in ways that are quiet, delicate, and subtle.

My experiences with the Spirit have most frequently been as Elder Bednar describes: quiet, delicate, and subtle. I also have occasionally received a personal witness of the power of the Holy Ghost in a more powerful fashion. Such was the case with an experience I had in which I came to understand more fully why we also refer to the Spirit as the Comforter:

As I was winding up my life in Connecticut, I began to look for a place to live in California. I attended general conference in Salt Lake City and then flew to Los Angeles that evening. When I landed, it was cold and rainy. I arrived at the house I had rented for a week and discovered that the owner, a commercial photographer of some repute, had used his gifts to greatest advantage in creating the photos of his home! The feeling of loneliness on that wearying night in that dreary house was almost physically heavy. I thought to myself, "What have I done? I've left a happy life in a beautiful place surrounded by people I love who also love me, and now I'm alone and miserable. Is this going to be my life?"

The only thing I could think to do was to fall on my knees and pour out my heart, my fear, my worries, and my distress. I am reminded of the scripture in Second Nephi that begins, "O how great the goodness of our God, who prepareth a way for our escape from the grasp of this awful monster" (2 Nephi 9:10), for in that instant I was flooded with a feeling of warmth and consolation.

Since that time, I have been struck again at unpredictable moments by that incredibly powerful desire to love and be loved by a unique other. In these moments, I have learned that when we speak of the Comforter, we are using a description that is literally accurate.

Brigham Young related a conversation with the martyred Joseph Smith in a vision:

> Tell the people to be humble and faithful and [be] sure to keep the Spirit of the Lord and it will lead them right. Be careful and not turn away the small still voice; it will teach [you what] to do and where to go; it will yield the fruits of the kingdom. Tell the brethren to keep their hearts open to conviction so that when the Holy Ghost comes to them, their hearts will be ready to receive it. They can tell the Spirit of the Lord from all other spirits. It will whisper peace and joy to their souls, and it will take malice, hatred, envying, strife, and all evil from their hearts; and their whole desire will be to do good, bring forth righteousness, and build up the kingdom of God. Tell the brethren if they will follow the Spirit of the Lord they will go right.

I hope that is a common experience for all of us, to know what it feels like when the Spirit whispers peace and joy to us. It is especially critical, I believe, for my LGBTQ brothers and sisters to know those feelings, to understand and recognize the presence of the Spirit in their lives in order to make the very best decisions they possibly can at each stage. I love the emphasis our Church places on personal revelation, on the opportunity and right each of us has to receive guidance from the Lord through the Spirit.

Elder Bruce R. McConkie, speaking at a BYU devotional, said:

> I desire to point attention to . . . the fact that revelation is not restricted to the prophet of God on earth. The visions of eternity are not reserved for Apostles—they are not reserved for the General Authorities. Revelation is something that should be received by every individual. . . . Our concern is to get personal revelation, to know for ourselves, independent of any other individual or set of individuals, what the mind and the will of the Lord is as pertaining to us in our individual concerns.

I am grateful for the experiences I have had to prophesy: "for the testimony of Jesus is the spirit of prophecy" (Revelation 19:10). "And Moses said unto him . . . would God that all the Lord's people were prophets, and that the Lord would put his spirit upon them!" (Numbers 11:29).

With Alma, I testify of the power of prophecy, the testimony of Christ, through the Holy Ghost:

> Do ye not suppose that I know of these things myself? Behold, I testify unto you that I do know that these

things whereof I have spoken are true. And how do ye suppose that I know of their surety?

Behold, I say unto you they are made known unto me by the Holy Spirit of God. Behold, I have fasted and prayed many days that I might know these things of myself. And now I do know of myself that they are true; for the Lord God hath made them manifest unto me by his Holy Spirit; and this is the spirit of revelation which is in me.

And moreover, I say unto you that it has thus been revealed unto me, that the words which have been spoken by our fathers are true, even so according to the spirit of prophecy which is in me, which is also by the manifestation of the Spirit of God. (Alma 5:45–47)

I witness that this great knowledge occurs not in ease and comfort but in the struggle to find meaning in the challenges and difficulties of our lives. This is a blessing I pray every one of my brothers and sisters will share in the fullest possible measure.

About a year after I had been baptized and had moved to California, one evening while driving from a conference I had a conversation with a person who has long been one of my heroes. I think it is fair to say that her life has been one long demonstration that love conquers all: she has yet to find anyone for whom she is unwilling to develop empathy. She has a first-rate mind and is gifted in the arts. Her kindness is legendary. From prior conversations, she knew how deeply I loved my partner and how keenly I felt our separation, especially knowing the pain and anger he experienced. She asked why I couldn't call him and find a way to be together again. I thought about her question for a few moments and finally said, "Because the way I feel now, the way

I experience the influence of the Holy Ghost, is powerful and delicious to me, and I don't ever want to live without it again. And, at least at this point, I don't see a way for us to be united in that effort." I have wondered if I had been a better example of the believers (see 1 Timothy 4:12), if that could have awakened a desire in my partner to understand and experience the confirming power of the Spirit and the redemptive and enabling powers of Christ's Atonement. I pray that someday he will know—and all who do not today share that awareness will know—the sweetness of communion with Heavenly Father and His Son through the Holy Spirit. To receive the ordinance bestowing the gift of the Holy Ghost has been for me the tenderest compensation for the changes I have made in my life, and I hope to live so that it always will be so.

The Character of Christ

In a conversation with my brother Todd in his office one day, he offered a poignant suggestion: that the study of the character of Christ could be an exercise in lifelong learning and would also prove helpful in my life as well as in opportunities to testify. I warmly endorse and pass along his suggestion, especially to my LGBTQ brothers and sisters and their parents. During times when we struggle to understand Heavenly Father's plan for us, we can find helpful insight when we focus on Christ. We can learn from His actions as well as His sermons and parables about the purpose of opposition, the difficult work of loving as He does, and the possibilities inherent in uniting our wills with His as His is aligned with that of the Father.

As Joseph Smith taught, "The fundamental principles of our

religion are the testimony of the Apostles and Prophets, concerning Jesus Christ, that He died, was buried, and rose again the third day, and ascended into heaven; and all other things which pertain to our religion are only appendages to it."

I aspire that we might find in the character of Jesus Christ attributes that call us to higher effort, greater commitment, and increased peace in each moment of our lives—attributes that enrich the lives of those we love and lift those we may never know. I share here a few of His characteristics that I have put together; you will likely have your own list, and other attributes will come to your mind that are meaningful to you. My experience is that each element becomes consequential when we have a trial that calls us to the Savior for that particular quality:

- We know that he is a Creator, having organized our earth, that "without him was not any thing made that was made" (John 1:1–5).
- Luke tells us, as part of the experience conversing with scholars in the temple when He was twelve, that "Jesus increased in wisdom and stature, and in favour with God and man" (Luke 2:52).
- John revealed that "he received not of the fulness at first, but continued from grace to grace, until he received a fulness; And thus he was called the Son of God, because he received not of the fulness at the first" (Doctrine and Covenants 93:13–14).
- He was a scholar. The Hebrew scriptures were a source of learning for Him, as demonstrated by His ability to cite passages from them. As recorded in the four gospels, He quotes Psalms eleven times, Deuteronomy on ten occasions, Isaiah eight times, and Exodus seven times.

- Jesus overcame temptations of His physical appetites, of wealth and power and pride (see Matthew 4:1–11).
- In His ministry, Jesus "went about doing good" (Acts 10:38).
- He watched over His sheep and had care for those who were lost (see Matthew 15:24; John 10:1–12).
- He demonstrated tender care for little children (see Mark 10:14; 3 Nephi 17:11–18).
- He relieved suffering and grief, healing the blind and deaf, those afflicted with palsy and leprosy, a man with a withered hand and a woman with "an issue of blood," the son of a nobleman, the servant of a centurion, a son with epilepsy; He raised from the dead the daughter of Jairus, the son of a widow in Nain, and Lazarus; He also performed similar miracles among the Nephites.
- He was willing to confront and correct hypocrisy (see Matthew 7:1–5, 15; 23:5, 23–32; Romans 12:9; 2 Corinthians 3:3–8).
- In His great intercessory prayer, Jesus acknowledged that His will is united with that of the Father, "That they all may be one; as thou, Father, art in me, and I in thee, that they also may be one in us: that the world may believe that thou hast sent me" (John 17:21).
- He was patient in trials, pain, and suffering, and willing to submit to His Father (see Matthew 26:39; Luke 22:42–44; Mark 14:34–36; Doctrine and Covenants 19:15–19).
- He is eager to forgive, promising to remember no more (interestingly, in the first of the various accounts of the First Vision, the Prophet Joseph relates that the Lord's

initial words were that his sins were forgiven) (see Luke 5:20–24; Matthew 9:2–7; Mark 2:5–12; Alma 24:10; Moroni 6:8; Doctrine and Covenants 1:32; 58:42–43).

- He knows the desires of our hearts (see Alma 41:5–6; 3 Nephi 9:20; Doctrine and Covenants 137:9).
- He comes to us where we are, such as with the Samaritan woman at Jacob's Well, she who had had five husbands and him whom she then had was not her husband (see John 4:5–26).
- He prays for us (see 3 Nephi 17:15–17).
- And always, always, He manifested particular care for the poor and needy, the downtrodden and marginalized, and called others to do the same (see Mark 1:40–42).

As members of The Church of Jesus Christ of Latter-day Saints, can anything be more crucial than to know whom we worship, lest we fall into the trap of worshipping what we have made ourselves? I think of the Apostle Paul, the only time he ever visited Athens, as he describes his trip to Mars Hill (Areopagus). He speaks of the citizens' fixation with "new things" and describes Athens as a "city wholly given to idolatry." With great power, Paul relates that journeying up the hill he had passed "an altar with this inscription, TO THE UNKNOWN GOD." To the people of Athens, Paul declares: "Whom therefore ye ignorantly worship, him declare I unto you." Testifying that the Lord created this world and everything in it, he cautions, "Neither is [the Lord] worshipped with men's hands, as though he needed any thing, seeing he giveth to all life, and breath, and all things"; rather all "should seek the Lord, if haply they might feel after him, and find him, though he be not far from every one of us: For in him we live, and move, and have our being" (Acts 17:16–28).

Paul's description, that we might "feel after him," resonates deeply with me. Our search to know the Savior involves both sustained intellectual effort and attention to what we feel through the Holy Ghost.

A friend whose generosity of spirit I deeply admire, Bob Rees, once said, "I distrust two kinds of Mormon: those who only think, and those who never think; I distrust two kinds of Mormon: those who only feel, and those who never feel; it is living the tension—any member of any religion will tell you if they are vitally engaged in that religion there is tension, and we can't escape it and so therefore we should embrace it. Christ's life is an embracing of tension, Christ's life is an embracing of paradox and conundra and enigma, it's trying to make things work that don't seem to work."

Attributed to Saint Augustine are the words, "Faith is to believe what you do not see; the reward of this faith is to see what you believe."

As we come to know who it is that we worship, faith can become knowledge. We often treat the word *faith* as a synonym for belief, but as I mentioned earlier, another similar concept is to substitute the word *loyalty*. I find that a very potent idea, that my expression of faith in the Lord is reflected in my loyalty to Him, in my willingness to follow even at times when I am "feeling after" in my search for answers.

President Gordon B. Hinckley pleaded:

> May the Lord bless us as builders of faith.
>
> May our testimonies strengthen and become as anchors to which others may secure their faith in hours of doubt and concern.
>
> May the candle of learning ever burn in our minds.

Above all, may testimony grow in our hearts that this is in reality the church of the living God and that it will continue to move forward to fulfill its divine destiny.

May we each do our part faithfully and with thanksgiving to the Lord for all the blessings he so wondrously bestows upon us as we follow his teachings and draw near to him.

I join President Hinckley in that prayer! I am reminded of the revelation that ingratitude and disobedience are the only ways man offends God (see Doctrine and Covenants 59:21). In my search for faithful solutions and my desire for consistent discipleship, I am reminded how generous the Lord has already been to me, how patiently and kindly He has led me each day, how the daily bread He has provided has allowed me to move toward Him. I am grateful to know that He will continue to offer those blessings, not just to me, but to all of His children.

We have no greater friend than Jesus Christ. He showed the greatest love as He laid down his life for us (see John 15:13). I have found that as I read, study, ponder, and pray to understand the love that motivated His Atonement, I begin to feel that I know Him. And yet I feel uncomfortable when the same language is used to describe a relationship with Christ as one would use speaking of a pal. I hope we never lose the feeling of reverence and awe for One who accomplished what no other could, whose gift, given freely to all who will receive it, can never be matched or earned. I know He lives because of the testimony I have received through the Holy Spirit.

CHAPTER 12

A Zion People

And the Lord called his people Zion,
because they were of one heart and one mind,
and dwelt in righteousness;
and there was no poor among them.
. . . for this is Zion—the pure in heart . . .

—MOSES 7:18; DOCTRINE AND COVENANTS 97:21

In December 2015, I received a call from Elder Christofferson. He said that as he was leaving a meeting, President Thomas S. Monson asked if he could stay for just a moment. President Monson then handed my brother an envelope and said that he would like Todd to take care of this matter personally. When Elder Christofferson opened the envelope, he saw that it contained instructions to restore my priesthood and temple blessings. We shed some tears together over the phone as we talked about a time to accomplish this ordinance. The following Sunday afternoon, I drove to Todd and Kathy's house. My brother Tim, his wife, Julie, and my brother Greg were in town and joined me there. And there, with just the six of us—and in the company of our parents, grandparents, and my sister-in-law MarJane from the other side of the veil—Elder Christofferson performed the blessing and pronounced glorious words of love, of encouragement, and of promise.

The following Sunday, I sat across the table from my stake president, Lew Cramer. Although I had been a member of his stake for less than a year, President Cramer had shown sincere kindness to me. His enthusiasm and eagerness to commence and complete my process to obtain a restoration of blessings enabling ... y as great as my own! I had ... e morning to gain his ap mentioned that President ... is meetings that morning. I waited to hear if my interview would be rescheduled but went to the stake president's office at the appointed time, just in case. President Cramer was there; though he was clearly not feeling well, he said this interview was too important to delay. After we had talked about the magnificent restoration blessing I had received, President Cramer began the first question, "Do you have faith . . ." That was all he could say before he was overcome with emotion. And for the next forty minutes, we shared our joyful witnesses of our Heavenly Father, of our Savior and Redeemer, and of His living servants, the prophets and apostles, as well as our gratitude for the blessing of making personal covenants with the Lord.

So many family members and dear friends had played significant roles in my journey of return that I had a difficult time narrowing down a list of people to invite to join me in my first temple session in three decades, which I scheduled for Thursday. Having a valid recommend in my wallet proved to be too great a temptation, though, and I quietly went through a session on

Tuesday in the Gilbert Arizona Temple and one on Wednesday in the Payson Utah Temple.

On Thursday, fifty friends and family members joined me in the Salt Lake Temple. Among those able to attend were my brothers and their wives, many of my nieces and nephews and their spouses, bishops, stake presidents, and counselors from New Canaan and Salt Lake City, and their wives, and beloved friends from many different times of my life.

I was struck as we sat in the session that accomplished men and women, people well-known in church and professional circles, in sports and business, sat in the same seats with all of the rest of us; there was no separation by position, wealth, or fame. We were as one, equal sons and daughters of our Heavenly Parents. At a certain point in the session, one man became ill and had to leave. The rest of us sat in silence waiting for him to return. It seemed a clear message that our company was not complete unless every individual was present, and we could not progress without each one participating in his or her sphere.

To me, that is a critical lesson as we seek to become a Zion people, united in hearts and minds in our love for the Savior. Every person is needed and wanted. The work of salvation and exaltation is essential for every one of us and requires every strength, talent, and capability that we have been given—and in that effort we sustain and support one another. The work of the Lord is incomplete until all have the opportunity to hear His voice and respond to His call. The greatest desire of His heart is that all—you, me, every member of our families, every person we love, as well as every other brother and sister in the family of God—all of us will come unto Him and gain all that is His to give. When we learn to care, as He does, for every individual, we understand that we cannot progress without each other. When we absorb that lesson and in turn desire with all our hearts that every person will receive every possible blessing of eternity, who we are is changed. We become like Him. Our hearts become Zion hearts.

Surely, as each one of us seeks discipleship, we recognize the requirement and opportunity to become one with each member of the family of God, to feed His sheep. The concept of Zion, of unity of purpose, with charity for all, is a sublime ideal. I believe we can move significantly closer to that state of harmony through selfless participation in our wards, stakes, and communities.

When the Saints of New Canaan welcomed both me and my partner to worship with them, to partake of the Spirit with them, to serve and share love with them, they did not impose a pre-qualification to work toward a specific outcome. Their actions reflected a deep faith that the will of the Lord can be made known in each person's life, and that the Spirit of the Lord will do His work in His own time and way. My partner and I were received as a couple and as individuals simply as we were. I want to be sure that those who read this book understand this point clearly: while not assuming that any other LGBTQ individual will see or follow exactly the way I have traversed, I am more grateful than words can express for the path that has been made available to me. I am thankful for the many people who are so important in my life, including my dear parents, and particularly for my partner, whose willingness to release me from commitments I had made to him allowed me to follow that path—one that in the following months would come to feel less joyful for him, and would cause him to decide to pursue his life separately.

Each of us is unique. Each of us has claim on our Heavenly Father for His inspiration and direction. Each of us is deserving of the love of our families and our congregations exactly as we are and where we are. The gifts of love, like the gift of the Resurrection, are offered freely and without condition. As we are able to fully feel the love of those around us and of the Lord, the love we feel in return will impel us to seek the Spirit in our lives, and that is a singular, unique process. I hope, as each of us strives to become one in purpose with our Savior, that we will open our hearts to everyone around us. I pray that our covenant to comfort anyone in need of comfort, our willingness to bear the burdens of others, will cause us to suspend judgment and cease putting prerequisites in the way of our sustaining support.

We learn in Zenos's allegory of the olive trees that the Lord of the vineyard tries over and over and over again to reach and save His precious fruit, His children. Of the lesson found in this allegory, Elder Jeffrey R. Holland has said, "At least fifteen times the Lord of the vineyard expresses a desire to bring the vineyard and its harvest to his 'own self,' and he laments no less than eight times, 'It grieveth me that I should lose this tree.' One student of the allegory says it should take its place beside the parable of the prodigal son, inasmuch as both stories 'make the Lord's mercy so movingly memorable.'"

By contrast, I have long been puzzled by the experience related in both the gospels of Matthew and Mark that took place the day after Christ's triumphant entrance into Jerusalem in the final week of His mortal life.

Now in the morning as he returned into the city, he hungered.

And when he saw a fig tree in the way, he came to it, and found nothing thereon, but leaves only, and said unto it, Let no fruit grow on thee henceforward for ever. And presently the fig tree withered away.

And when the disciples saw it, they marvelled, saying, How soon is the fig tree withered away! (Matthew 21:18–20)

Explanations I have heard over the years related these passages to an object lesson on hypocrisy, likening the appearance of leaves on the barren tree (which would normally indicate fruit is present) to persons who put forth an appearance of righteousness while being inwardly corrupt. And although the lessons taught by the Savior operate on many levels, and over time we can find different and perhaps deeper meanings as we gain experience in our own lives, nonetheless it has seemed to me to be out of character for Jesus to cause a living thing to perish.

I am indebted to my friend Micah Christensen for pointing me toward the fourth-century writings of Ephrem the Syrian, who indicated that in the cultural understanding of the time, as the owner of the tree was harvesting its fruit, he should have left some on the tree for the disadvantaged and for travelers. "The owner of the fig tree did not obey the law but spurned it. Our Lord came and found that there was nothing left on it, so he cursed it, lest its owner eat from it again, since he had left nothing for the orphan and widows." We know the earth will, in due time, be exalted, and I wonder if causing the tree to wither, a temporary sacrifice, is in fact another example of the efforts the Lord makes to reach and to invite His people to come unto Him. Losing a tree may have been costly to the owner, but this reminder of the great commandments to love God and serve His children may have provided an opportunity to reflect and change course.

In my vision of a Zion congregation, I see the Lord's patience demonstrated through the sincere goodwill and fellowship for same-sex couples and their families, for former members, for those whose foundation of faith has crumbled, for the poor in spirit as well as the needy in terms of the things of this world. A city or congregation of Zion is a place of learning, a place of culture and the arts, a place of laughter and joy. A place of gratitude for the incomparable gifts of grace and mercy. A place of growth and of journeys in process. A place to be nurtured and a place to contribute.

In his remarkable sermon on charity (see 1 Corinthians 13), Paul teaches of this Zion responsibility: to bless the lives of all who surround us, seeking the gift of charity, which is the essential trait of a Christian. I have found that it is nearly impossible to be filled with charity for others if I have not understood that charity is also the defining characteristic of how my Heavenly Father engages with me. As with the prophet Jeremiah, so also with us: "Before I formed thee in the belly I knew thee" (Jeremiah 1:5). Until we recognize that He who knows us best also loves us most, we are likely to spin our wheels, failing to gain traction in our life's work, which is to prepare for the ultimate journey of returning to Him.

Because Christ said to his Nephite disciples, "What manner of men ought ye to be? Verily I say unto you, even as I am" (3 Nephi 27:27), or to those in Galilee hearing the Sermon on the Mount, "Be ye therefore perfect, even as your Father which is in heaven is perfect" (Matthew 5:48), we sometimes conclude that perfection—living without sin—is meant to be our earthly objective, and our way to have the Lord to be our God. President Russell M. Nelson taught us to be more realistic about those whom the scriptures characterize as perfect, and therefore about our expectations of ourselves. "Scriptures have described Noah, Seth, and Job as *perfect* men. No doubt the same term might apply to a large number of faithful disciples in various dispensations," but that "does not mean that these people never made mistakes or never had need of correction." I have appreciated President Nelson's insights, together with an understanding of Old Testament scriptures that complete loyalty to Jehovah, according to Professor Frank Judd Jr., is not achieved "by simply keeping all the commandments. In the context of the story [of the rich young man], as an upstanding Jew who kept the Ten Commandments, the young man would have already likely made it a practice to give some of his wealth to those in need. But that past obedience was not enough to achieve perfection or completeness. The heart [or meaning] of perfection is true discipleship; it is following the Savior."

The traditional reading of the story of Jesus's encounter with the rich young man—or the rich young ruler, as he is alternatively called—is that his love for his possessions exceeded his desire to do all that God might command. Another possible reading, though, is that this worthy, obedient person who had kept the commandments since his youth was seeking an additional list of performances to certify his worthiness, misunderstanding that the gospel of Jesus Christ seeks to change our actions predominantly as a means to change our hearts.

In our quest for discipleship, perhaps we could stop seeing commandments as a list of performances, each of which must be perfectly accomplished every day. Remembering President Dieter F. Uchtdorf's insight that "Salvation cannot be bought with the currency of obedience; it is purchased by the blood of the Son of God," it might be helpful to consider the impact of how we focus our efforts.

If our sole or primary focus in becoming a disciple of Jesus Christ is to *live* perfectly, to observe every performance and commandment perfectly, we are likely to discover that we turn inward. Our focus is on ourselves, on what and how we are doing, and in that self-assessment mode it is almost inevitable that we will come to compare our efforts to those of others. We may discover pride when we feel that our efforts are surpassing those of others around us. We may discover envy when we feel that our efforts are falling short of those around us. We will likely ignore what the Lord has told us, that our intentions and desires are at least as important as our actions. We may become hypercritical of ourselves. Said Elder Neal A. Maxwell, "Some of us stand before no more harsh a judge than ourselves, a judge who stubbornly refuses to admit much happy evidence and who cares nothing for due process."

However, if our primary focus and object in life is to *love* perfectly, then we may discover all the Savior was striving to teach us about contrite and ultimately changed hearts: "Thou shalt love the Lord thy God with all thy heart, and with all thy soul, and with all thy mind. This is the first and great commandment. And the second is like unto it, Thou shalt love thy neighbour as thyself. On these two commandments hang all the law and the prophets" (Matthew 22:37–40).

"By this shall all men know that ye are my disciples, if ye have love one to another" (John 13:35).

"I know thy heart, and have heard thy prayers concerning thy brethren . . . let thy love be for them as for thyself; and let thy love abound unto all men" (Doctrine and Covenants 112:11).

"We love him, because he first loved us" (1 John 4:19).

When we seek to love perfectly, our focus is outward. We strive to learn what it is that God loves about each one of His children. Knowledge of our own shortcomings creates a humble desire to aid, to lift, to serve a brother or sister in need.

As the Apostle Paul wrote to his brothers and sisters in the Roman church, "For all have sinned, and come short of the glory of God; being justified freely by his grace through the redemption that is in Christ Jesus" (Romans 3:23–24).

When our primary focus is to love perfectly, the crucial elements of living perfectly naturally come along: humility, hope, patience, faith, kindness, consideration, courtesy, care, laughter, unselfishness, prayer, thoughtfulness, forgiving one another, sustaining one another, and, above all, the gift of charity, "and whoso is found possessed of it at the last day, it shall be well with him" (Moroni 7:47).

When we understand that the purpose of commandments, of the performances of the law, is to bring our hearts to Christ, to give us greater desire and greater capacity to be imbued with the first and second great commandments, then we become pliable in the Savior's hands to do His work in His way. We lose a sense of competition with other disciples and gain an awareness of our supporting role in the Savior's work: "to bring to pass the immortality and eternal life of man" (Moses 1:39).

Alma offers us some timeless questions to gauge our progress: "And now behold, I ask of you, my brethren [and sisters] of the church, have ye spiritually been born of God? Have ye received his image in your countenances? Have ye experienced this mighty change in your hearts?" (Alma 5:14). I know it is His desire to bless us with changed hearts, hearts upon which He has written

His law with His love, if we will but let Him enter (see Jeremiah 31:33, Romans 2:15, Hebrews 10:16).

As our hearts are becoming changed, we as members of a Zion family and a Zion congregation will seek and find opportunities to celebrate the same process in the lives of those around us, at whatever stage of that undertaking they may be.

When we as LGBTQ/SSA individuals seek Heavenly Father's counsel, I believe He can help us learn to use those experiences that have brought understanding and wisdom to our lives, as well as some of the attributes and traits that accompany us in this life, to aid us in our quest to become like His Son. You and I can see that "all these things shall give [us] experience, and shall be for [our] good" (Doctrine and Covenants 122:7), that because of our experiences we can be more sensitive to the challenges of others, more willing to pardon, more eager to encourage, more determined to avoid judging. The Prophet Joseph Smith said: "Don't be limited in your views with regard to your neighbors' virtues. . . . You must enlarge your souls toward others if you [would] do like Jesus. . . . As you increase in innocence and virtue, as you increase in goodness, let your hearts expand—let them be enlarged towards others—you must be longsuffering and bear with the faults and errors of mankind. How precious are the souls of men!"

As we strive to be like Jesus, we can be diligent in seeking out those who seem alone or uncomfortable in our wards and taking the initiative to make them feel welcome. We can choose our own "home teaching routes" as we pray to recognize the needs of others. And as we recognize the imperative in Jesus's question, "And if ye salute your brethren only, what do ye more than others?" (Matthew 5:47), we can be first to utter the kind word, first to offer praise, last to criticize or find fault.

The experience of "coming out," or of having a child "come out," or of being a ward member or leader who becomes aware of an LGBTQ member in his or her stewardship, can teach us that we are capable of greater empathy, understanding, compassion, and charity than we had previously imagined. As recipients of that gift, we will likely discover that there are so many others around us, far beyond the LGBTQ community, who will flourish when receiving our expansive acceptance and embrace. Zion is incomplete until each child of God joins us.

I find myself a member of two tribes. I love equally my lesbian, gay, bisexual, transgender, and queer brothers and sisters, as well as my fellow Latter-day Saints, and I so desperately want each to love and esteem the other. I love my Mormon brothers and sisters for their eagerness to help one another and the wider world; I love them for their devotion to duty; I love their decency and their reverence for things sacred. I love my queer brothers and sisters for their zest for life; I love their humor and sensitivity to others; I love that they seek fairness for all; I love their loyalty and their optimism for a better tomorrow. This Zion we are venturing to create needs all of these strengths and all of these gifts. Every individual is needed and wanted in His kingdom.

I am grateful for the wisdom, patience, perseverance, and charity of my parents. Their gentle goodness, their overarching faith, their willingness to be guided and to grow created a climate of Zion in our home. I am indebted to bishops and stake presidents whose humanity, whose love for the Savior's mercy, whose eagerness to learn, and whose determination to follow the Spirit encourage Zion to blossom. I offer grateful praise for the goodness of the members of wards who have loved me and shared my delight in newfound understanding. I am beholden to four magnificent brothers whose affection has never wavered and whose diligent discipleship continues to beckon me to greater energy and more consistent commitment as I endeavor to follow their quiet examples of charity.

I am humbled by the goodness of our God. I am astounded by the supreme love and watchcare of my Savior. I stand in grateful awe of His grace. I have been blessed beyond any possible relation to my own efforts, blessed by a family and by congregations that have helped me to be one with them, to witness daily devotion to Christ and His gospel. Above all, I have been blessed through the gift of the Spirit, to feel one with my Heavenly Father and my Redeemer. I pray that this blessing of unity will prevail not only for all of my LGBTQ brothers and sisters but for all the children of God—"that we may be one" (3 Nephi 19:23).

Author's Note

As you have discovered, I am not a psychiatrist or a trained mental-health professional. I am not a General Authority. I do not hold myself out as a role model. I am not a professional speaker or motivator or coach. I am not even a parent.

I have become converted to the gospel of Jesus Christ and to The Church of Jesus Christ of Latter-day Saints. I am simply one who aspires to become a steady and trustworthy disciple of my Lord. I am a son, a brother, an uncle, a friend.

Each of us will experience our path of conversion in uniquely individual ways, and yet I hope that the perspectives and experiences that I have shared here will be useful to at least some of the people who read this book. As John Donne wrote, "No man is an island entire of itself; every man is a piece of the continent, a part of the main." The stories those I have met have shared with me have enriched my understanding and nourished my soul. I hope my journey and my story will likewise prove useful to some of those who read it.

To say that I am grateful to my noble parents and their parents; to my wonderful aunts, uncles, and Christofferson and Swenson cousins; to my magnificent brothers, their wives, and my beloved nieces and nephews, is to faintly praise those to whom I owe nearly everything in my life. Their unqualified love and constant support, their patience and watchcare, their goodness and generosity are a source of constant blessings to me. I wish my parents were still living: the book they could have written would far surpass this one.

Each of my brothers and sisters-in-law read various versions of this manuscript, and each provided helpful recollections and clarifications. All have made this endeavor the beneficiary of their interest and prayers. I hope in your reading you have gained some sense of the superb people they are. If so, you will understand the sheer delight I take in their company and recognize how incredibly fortunate I am to share a life with them.

I have also been blessed with more splendid friends than anyone should reasonably expect. Many of them have read versions of the book and likewise provided helpful ideas and suggestions. (I would have been wise to incorporate more of them.) I begin with my dear sisters of the DC Brigade: Tammy Maxwell, Alyson Powers Deussen, Kathryn Hueth, and Kit Hunt. Other friends donated time and intellect to this project, among them (and with apologies to those I have neglected to mention): Barb and Steve Young, Jonathan and Rachel Manwaring, Gretchen and Chuck (Chip) Terry, and Nina Brostrum. A lifelong friend whose erudition and humble pastoral care are exemplary, Richard Neitzel Holzapfel, graciously read early drafts and provided encouragement to continue. A few dear friends who have, in their own ways, walked paths that have likewise brought them home were careful readers of the first draft and kindly shared their perspectives, which have enriched mine: Jamison Manwaring, Melinda Evans, Rod Olson, and especially Maxine Hanks. I will forever be grateful for the guides who so gently and lovingly walked side by side with me, without whom I likely might not have arrived at this point: the members and leaders of the New Canaan Ward and the Yorktown New York Stake. Bishop Bruce Larson and President Dave Checketts read the first draft of the manuscript and helped me remember additional experiences that illuminate these pages. My debt to them goes far beyond publishing a book—they and their wives, Gayle Larson and Deb Checketts, have taught me what it means to minister, to be a shepherd.

My thanks to my friends at Deseret Book: Sheri Dew, Emily Watts, and Laurel Christensen Day, who thought there could be an opportunity to make more fruitful the conversation between Church members and their LGBTQ brothers and sisters, and who have with kindness and humor borne the challenge of working with a first-time author. That you were even aware this book existed is testament to the abilities of Laurel Day and her team! Any parts of the book that seem to have a coherent flow are due to the efforts of editor Emily Watts; the rest of the book is mine. Emily made this process such a pleasant experience that I wish I had a second book in me! Anything in the book that seems to be at odds with sagacious and inspired leaders is my sole responsibility; the parts that harmonize with good teaching reflect the gentle guidance of Sheri Dew. The process of creating this book has allowed me to deepen my friendship with Sheri, for which I am enormously grateful. I am in awe of her ability to listen, absorb, and find nuggets of value in every conversation and engagement.

Members of the Backsliders book group have graciously taken in a wandering orphan, and I have repaid their kindness by tormenting them with every excruciating detail of this book. My love and thanks to Suzanne Stott, Linda Williams-Evans, Jeff Johnson, Linda Charney, Esther and Kirk Henrichsen, and Anny

Opfar. Your one consolation is that I won't propose we put this book on our reading list!

My life has been enriched and my understanding expanded by the opportunity to know and claim as friends three remarkable individuals: Carol Lynn Pearson, Darius Gray, and Bill Evans. Each has lived a life wherein the pure love of Christ has been evident. Their courage and intelligence, together with that charity, have caused many minds and hearts to expand; each has helped fellow Church members see with new eyes, with vision sharpened by added compassion and wider perception. Although they have not been directly associated with this book, I hope that some of the poignant lessons I have learned from associating with them will have found some reflection here.

Notes

Introduction

page xvi, "time's best jewel," William Shakespeare, Sonnet 65.

Chapter 1

page 3, "Apart from the pulling and hauling," Walt Whitman, "Song of Myself, IV" (1892).

page 9, "In the heav'ns are parents single?," "O My Father," *Hymns of The Church of Jesus Christ of Latter-day Saints* [1985], no. 292.

Chapter 2

page 10, "The joys of parents," Francis Bacon, "Of Parents and Children," *Essays, Civil and Moral.*

page 11, "In 1960, I was fifteen," in Richard Swenson, editor, "Adena Hannah Warnick Swenson and Helge Vincent Swenson," unpublished manuscript (1993), 106.

page 12, "Through one particular instance," ibid., 96–97.

page 14, "Years ago, when my brothers and I were boys," D. Todd Christofferson, "Let Us Be Men," *Ensign,* November 2006.

page 16, "Tom called me from Los Angeles one day," email to author from Greg Christofferson; used with permission.

page 20, "One with her are mirth and duty," William Butler Yeats, "A Dream of a Blessed Spirit" (1921).

Chapter 3

page 21, "There is a tide in the affairs of men," William Shakespeare, *Julius Caesar,* act 4, scene 3, lines 224–30.

page 22, "There is no pain so awful," in Andrew F. Ehat and

Lyndon W. Cook, eds., *The Words of Joseph Smith: The Contemporary Accounts of the Nauvoo Discourses of the Prophet Joseph* (1980), 183.

page 25, "Jesus did not commence the conversation," Camille Fronk Olson, *Women of the New Testament* (2014), 222, 225.

page 27, "As a companion to that love," Richard G. Scott, "'I Have Given You an Example,'" *Ensign*, May 2014.

page 27, "Being content," Neal A. Maxwell, "Content with the Things Allotted unto Us," *Ensign*, May 2000.

Chapter 4

page 29, "These weary hours will not be lost," Anne Brontë, "Last Lines" (1849).

page 30, "more than 400,000 U.S. service members would be killed," see "World War II casualties," Wikipedia.

page 30, "I am praying with all my heart," Heber J. Grant, in Conference Report, October 1944, 10.

page 30, "Don't try to live too many days ahead," Harold B. Lee, in Conference Report, October 1970, 117–18.

page 30, "Thoughtful planning and preparation are key," D. Todd Christofferson, "Give Us This Day Our Daily Bread," Church Educational System Fireside, January 9, 2011.

page 32, "Remember then," Leo Tolstoy, "Three Questions," in *Twenty-Three Tales*, trans. L. and A. Maude (1907).

page 32, "I was so sick and weak," Jeanne S. Christoffersen, unpublished manuscript.

page 34, "Our trusting contentment," Neal A. Maxwell, "Content with the Things Allotted unto Us," *Ensign*, May 2000.

page 35, "Just as the capacity to defer," Neal A. Maxwell, "'Willing to Submit,'" *Ensign*, May 1985.

page 38, "When you climb up a ladder," *Teachings of Presidents of the Church: Joseph Smith* (2007), 268.

page 40, "What praises can we offer," "O Savior, Thou Who Wearest a Crown," *Hymns*, no. 197.

Chapter 5

page 42, "There's a wideness in God's mercy," Frederick William Faber, "There's a Wideness in God's Mercy" (1862).

page 50, "My own Warnick ancestors," see Gregory P. Christofferson, "The Warnicke Family: A Prototype of Mormon Emigration from Scandinavia in the 1860s," unpublished manuscript, 2000.

Chapter 6

page 54, "Know this, that ev'ry soul is free," *Hymns*, no. 240.

page 55, "At the zenith of His mortal ministry," Jeffrey R. Holland, "The Cost—and Blessings—of Discipleship," *Ensign*, May 2014; emphasis in original.

page 59, "In reality, the best way to help those we love," D. Todd Christofferson, "Saving Your Life," Church Educational System Fireside, September 14, 2014.

page 60, "This son's sexual orientation," Jeffrey R. Holland, "Behold Thy Mother," *Ensign*, November 2015.

page 60, "We needed to stop asking," Victor Frankl, *Man's Search for Meaning* (Beacon Press, 2006), 77.

page 62, "He who judges perfectly," funeral address given by author, 2016.

page 65, "Effective loving is far more," H. Wallace Goddard and Larry C. Jensen, "Understanding and Applying Proclamation Principles of Parenting," in David C. Dollahite, D.C., ed., *Strengthening Our Families: An In-Depth Look at the Proclamation on the Family* (2000), 125. Information on the Family Acceptance Project can be found at https://familyproject.sfsu.edu.

Chapter 7

page 69, "'Hope' is the thing with feathers—," Emily Dickinson, Sonnet 254.

page 72, "Howard W. Hunter was raised," *Teachings of Presidents of the Church: Howard W. Hunter* (2015), 197.

page 75, "As we grow in the gospel," Robert D. Hales, *Return: Four Phases of Our Mortal Journey Home* (2010), 87–88.

page 76, "The precise nature of the test of mortality," David A. Bednar, "We Believe in Being Chaste," *Ensign*, May 2013.

Chapter 8

page 80, "All paths that have been, or should be," "Gethsemane," Ella Wheeler Wilcox (1887).

page 80, "in the quiet heart," "Savior, May I Learn to Love Thee," *Hymns*, no. 220.

page 83, ". . . that all/The terrors," William Wordsworth, "The Prelude: Book 1" (1888).

page 85, "Service ever was their watchcry," "They, the Builders of the Nation," *Hymns*, no. 36.

page 85, "One of the most significant ways," Jean B. Bingham, "I Will Bring the Light of the Gospel Into My Home," *Ensign*, November 2016.

Chapter 9

page 93, "Brightly beams our Father's mercy," *Hymns*, no. 335.

page 96, "On the first night that we met," letter to author from Bruce M. Larson, March 26, 2014; used with permission.

page 99, "no more a stranger," Isaac Watts, "My Shepherd Will Supply My Need"; see also Ephesians 2:19; Psalm 23.

page 104, "as you submit your wills to God," Neal A. Maxwell, "Remember How Merciful the Lord Hath Been," *Ensign*, May 2004.

page 104, "All the principles and ordinances," Harold B. Lee, *Stand Ye In Holy Places* (1974), 215.

page 105, "The love [of] the Savior," M. Russell Ballard, "Finding Joy through Loving Service," *Ensign*, May 2011.

Chapter 10

page 106, "In this Church there are no strangers and no outcasts," Gérald Caussé, "Ye Are No More Strangers," *Ensign*, November 2013.

page 110, "Now I come before the altar," Annette W. Dickman, "Bread of Life, Living Water," *Ensign,* July 2015.

page 111, "The Church is a home for all," Dieter F. Uchtdorf, "Receiving a Testimony of Light and Truth," *Ensign*, November 2014.

page 113, "As surely as the rescue of those in need," Jeffrey R. Holland, "Prophets in the Land Again," *Ensign*, November 2006.

page 115, "Life is perfect for none of us," Thomas S. Monson, "Charity Never Faileth," *Ensign*, November 2010; emphasis in original.

Chapter 11

page 117, "Pale the sky, first stars appear," Lorene de St. Aubin, "By Winter's Morning Light"; used by permission.

page 118, "pure intelligence," *Teachings of Presidents of the Church: Joseph Smith* (2007), 132.

page 118, "We can, if we live worthy of it," Henry B. Eyring, "The Holy Ghost as Your Companion," *Ensign*, November 2015.

page 120, "When I was a young man," Heber J. Grant, *Gospel Standards,* comp. G. Homer Durham (1941), 294–95.

page 122, "Strong, dramatic spiritual impressions," David A. Bednar, "That We May Always Have His Spirit to Be with Us," *Ensign*, May 2006.

page 123, "Tell the people to be humble and faithful," *Teachings: Joseph Smith* (2007), 98.

page 124, "I desire to point attention," Bruce R. McConkie, BYU Devotional, October 11, 1966; published as "How to Get Personal Revelation," *New Era,* June 1980.

page 126, "The fundamental principles of our religion," *Teachings: Joseph Smith,* 49.

page 127, "He quotes Psalms eleven times," see Jeffrey Kranz, "Which Old Testament Book Did Jesus Quote Most," *biblia .com,* April 30, 2014, http://blog.biblia.com/2014/04/which-old -testament-book-did-jesus-quote-most/.

page 128, "He relieved suffering and grief," see "The Healings of Jesus

NOTES

Christ," *stronginfaith.org,* copyright 2007, http://stronginfaith.org
/article.php?page=9; see also 3 Nephi 17:7–10.

page 128, "interestingly, in the first of the various accounts," see www
.josephsmithpapers.org/paper-summary/history-circa-summer-1832/3.

page 130, "I distrust two kinds of Mormon," Dr. Robert A. Rees and
Dr. Gina Colvin, *A Thoughtful Faith* podcast, 086, January 16, 2015.

page 130, "May the Lord bless us as builders of faith," Gordon B.
Hinckley, "Go Forward with Faith," *Ensign,* August 1986.

Chapter 12

page 136, "At least fifteen times," Jeffrey R. Holland, *Christ and the
New Covenant* (1997), 165.

page 137, "The owner of the fig tree," Chester Beatty, trans. *Saint
Ephrem's Commentary on Tatian's Diatessaron: An English Translation*
(1993), 245–47.

page 139, "Scriptures have described Noah," Russell M. Nelson,
"Perfection Pending," *Ensign,* November 1995, emphasis in original.

page 139, "by simply keeping all the commandments," Frank F. Judd,
Jr., "'Be Ye Therefore Perfect': The Elusive Quest for Perfection," in
*The Sermon on the Mount in Latter-day Scripture: The 39th Annual
BYU Sidney B. Sperry Symposium,* edited by Gaye Strathearn,
Thomas A. Wayment, and Daniel L. Belnap (2010).

page 139, "Salvation cannot be bought," Dieter F. Uchtdorf, "The
Gift of Grace," *Ensign,* May 2015.

page 140, "Some of us stand," Neal A. Maxwell, "Notwithstanding
My Weakness," *Ensign,* November 1976.

page 142, "Don't be limited in your views," Joseph Smith, in *Daughters
in My Kingdom: The History and Work of Relief Society* (2011), 23.

Author's Note

page 145, "No man is an island," John Donne, "Meditation XVII,"
Devotions upon Emergent Occasions (1624).

Tom Christofferson has spent his career in investment management and asset servicing, living in the United States and Europe. He has served as a director on corporate and nonprofit boards and was a founding board member of Encircle, a group providing resources to support LGBTQ individuals and their families in Provo, Utah. Tom is an active member of The Church of Jesus Christ of Latter-day Saints and serves as a Gospel Doctrine teacher in his Salt Lake City ward.

Tom can be reached at ThatWeMayBeOne@gmail.com